Feb. 10, 1997

BAIL-OUT!

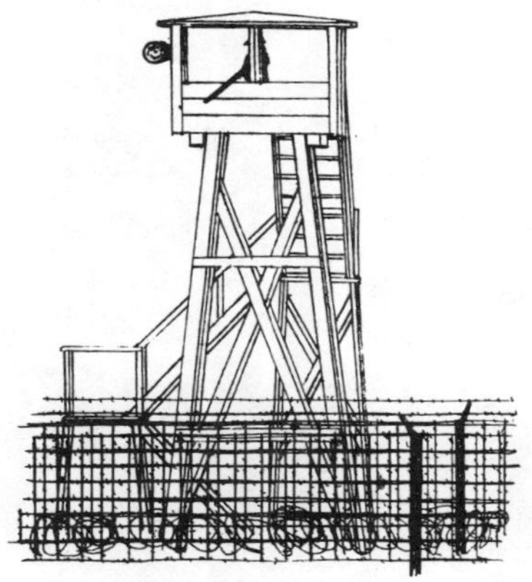

A view from our window.

Bail-Out!

POW, 1944-1945

Mel TenHaken

Sunflower University Press®
1531 Yuma (Box 1009), Manhattan, Kansas 66502-4228 USA

ISBN 0-89745-129-5

Line drawings by Mel TenHaken

Edited by Abigail Siddall

Layout by Lori L. Daniel

To all of those who never got the chance to return home and tell their stories.

A B-24 of the 15th AF. (Courtesy Bob McGuire, Liberator Club, San Diego, CA)

Contents

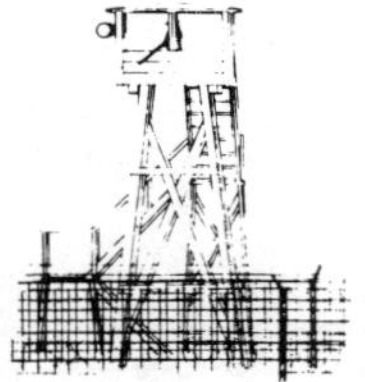

Preface

My intent throughout the following story has been to relate facts and sequences as I perceived them when they occurred. Conversations are quoted verbatim when known; they are otherwise presented as best remembered to portray incidents in the way they were seen and heard.

Because I knew none of the non-English languages encountered in Europe, I have used English phonetic spelling to convey my impression of what Germans, Yugoslavians, Italians, and others were saying to me.

Actual names are used only for those persons who were internationally known; all others are changed, because the only object here is a valid narrative of our experiences and our responses.

Words used to describe emotions and reactions are those of the World War II era; I do not feel that I have negative personal attitudes or biases against present-day individuals or their governments because of that war.

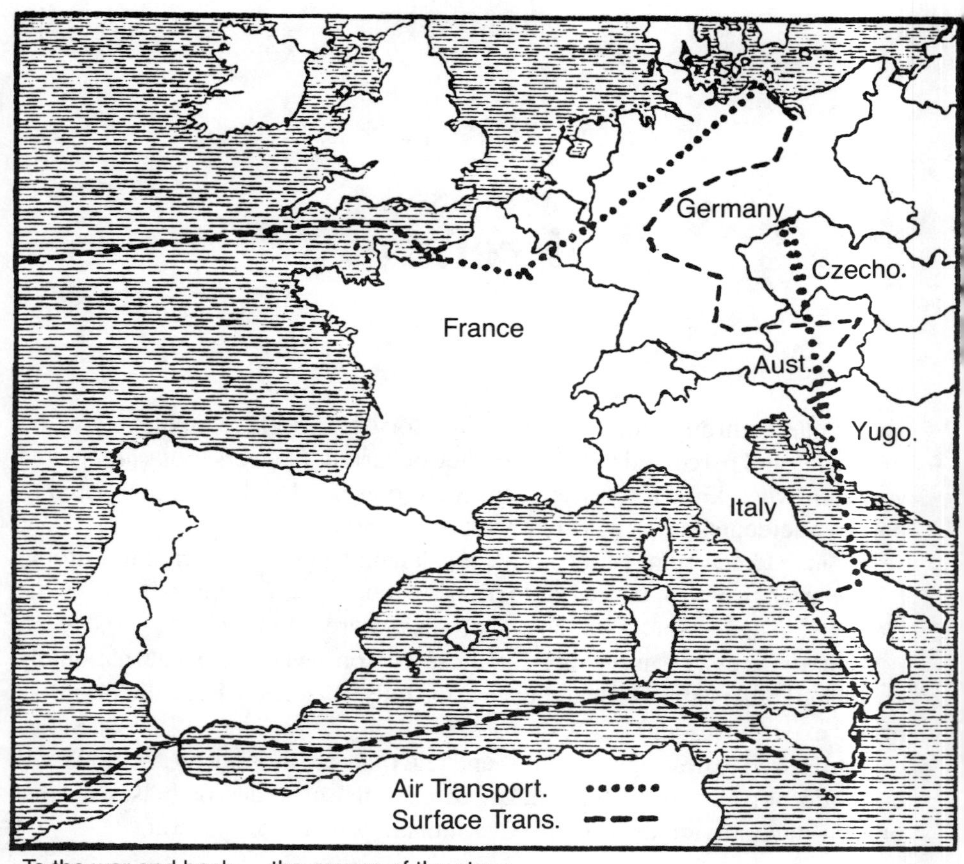

To the war and back — the course of the story.

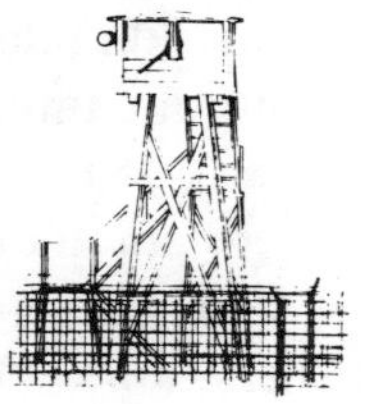

Chapter 1

Where Have All the Nazis Gone?

A group of American former prisoners of war recently invited a fellow citizen to speak at their monthly meeting because he, some forty years earlier at the age of twenty, had been a Luftwaffe pilot. In his speech he explained what he knew about tactics used in the German war effort, related personal experiences from that era, and repeatedly stressed the one point he wanted to be sure was understood: "I, of course, was never a Nazi."

His emphasis of that point reminded me that I, some forty years earlier at the age of twenty, had been in a jail cell in Ljubljana, Yugoslavia, where a captor had proudly stressed the *counter* point because, at that time, he wanted to be sure that *that* was understood: "I, of course, am a Nazi."

There were eight of us in the jail cell. We had met the Nazi four days earlier when he had interrogated each of us. We were desperately hungry after only a noon serving each day of unseasoned cabbage leaves floating in a cup of the water they had been boiled in.

We had talked very little, because we suspected there were microphones concealed in the cell; but also because our thoughts were convoluting collages of flak-bursts in the black cloud we had flown through above the target in Czechoslovakia, the bailout over Yugoslavia, and subsequent ground scenes leading to our imprisonment.

We remained tense. The cots were angle-iron racks with thin, stiff mats which had a noisy pine-needle filling: some of us tried not to move during the night in case someone was sleeping.

A faint clicking sound had concerned me the first night. When I discerned that our upper turret gunner was sliding beads on his rosary, I was glad he was on the cot next to mine where he wouldn't disturb the others. That reasoning comforted me until the wee hours toward morning when the lower ball gunner snarled from across the room, "Can't you stop jangling that goddam chain?"

A makeshift board wall and a curtain in one corner of the room shrouded our toilet, which was a twenty-gallon caldron identical to the one our cabbage soup was carried in. Other prisoners came in to serve from one and empty the other while German guards muttered guttural obscenities at them.

There was no sign of decency or dignity. We had watched through the bars of our third-floor window the previous day as a team of horses drew a low wagon bearing two casket-shaped boxes into our half-acre courtyard — rough boards had been sawed and nailed to the right shape and size. The boxes were backed to a service door and slid down to the entrance way, bodies of former prisoners were flung into the boxes, and within seconds they were hoisted back onto the wagons — and there was space in the jail for more prisoners.

To nurture that essence of life called hope, one must be able to look forward. We could not imagine a future. There were only the dirty gray plaster walls; the recent past was confusion, and other attempts to think seemed void.

But then there was a metallic clatter at the lock of the heavy door, and our interrogator strode into our cell. With the rich black of his uniform, the bits of cardinal decoration, the reflections from his silver medals, the shine from his boots, the click from his heel plates — his appearance was resplendent.

We had hated him — and then blocked him out of our memory.

Each in turn, prior to the interrogation, had been "inspected" by his goons. While we stood naked, they had fingered through our rectums, our scrotums, our armpits, our ears, our hair, and our mouths, purportedly looking for evidence of spy activity. Then we had been ordered to put on our undershorts in respect for the interrogator.

After our salute and report of name, rank, and service serial number, each of us had stood at a ludicrous, shivering form of attention. His index finger made a slashing motion across his throat to demonstrate what he would have someone do to us if we couldn't offer adequate information to clear ourselves from suspected spy efforts. I presumed that each of us wondered about the patriotic fidelity of the others when the German claimed they had all yielded far more than the minimum identification.

But now he was friendly. He smiled. He just wanted to talk. When he took a cigarette pack from his pocket, we knew our desire for tobacco smoke was probably as desperate as that for food. While carefully noting our insignia, he offered them, first to the flight officer, then to the staff sergeant, and then to the corporals. He lit them in the same order.

He reiterated that he wanted this to be casual. He had some questions, but they involved only personal thoughts. The interrogation was over. He hoped our answers might clarify some of his concerns. Then:

"Why are you fighting this war?"

After random glances, he fixed a quizzical gaze toward our flight officer. Then, in order of rank, he received eight shrugs.

I knew I had a valid excuse for my shrug because we had been told that, in case of capture, communication with the enemy must be restricted to a respectful salute and report of name, rank, and serial number. But I was also bewildered by the sudden realization that we had never asked ourselves that question.

After a disquieting silence, he suggested it might be easier to begin with a different approach:

"Who do you think will win the war?"

He seemed pleased when, after more shrugs and silence, our tail turret gunner quietly returned the question. Our interrogator straightened his posture and opened with the statement which he appeared to feel would validate everything he would say:

"I, of course, am a Nazi."

He was confident that they would win the war. He explained there was something he would have to tell us about because it had begun on 16 December, the day they had shot our plane down "along with many, many others." Three of Field Marshal von Rundstedt's armies had opened a major offensive along a 150-kilometer front toward the west. Very little resistance was being encountered. Over 100 kilometers had already been secured in their drive to the edge of the continent. Many hundreds, perhaps thousands, of American troops had been taken prisoner.

We were skeptical of his report, but weeks later we learned he had described quite accurately what was to become famous as "the Battle of the Bulge," the last concerted effort of the Third Reich to turn the war's tide before its five-month sweep toward Berlin.

"Yes," he continued. "There is reason to feel we will win the war in the normally accepted sense. But the term '*win*' would require further definition, and that is more to the substance of my first question.

"You see, some very unfortunate turns have occurred in these recent years. Ignoring the insignificant countries, essentially we now find Germany, Italy, and Japan fighting England, America, and the Soviet Union. This is mere chaos. Neither side can now accomplish a useful win. If we win this war, so to speak, we will have to fight the Japanese; if you should win, you would have to fight the Russians — eventually at least, in either case.

"Hitler had a superb plan. And he used his own initiative to attempt to implement it. He always felt America, some day, if aid were necessary, would assist in our effort to save the world from Bolshevism. He was very disheartened when your country entered the war against us — we all were.

"You see, what should have happened is this: Germany, England, and

America should have fought Russia, Italy and Japan. Then we could have accomplished something! The world's better people, if you will, the more capable people, would then be making decisions for those less able to determine a best course."

He looked about for comments. There were only more shrugs. He was sorry we were unwilling to voice our opinions. He informed us we would be moved the next day. He seemed less confident when he turned at the door with a slight farewell smile.

The night was sleepless again, but there was reason to try to hope; perhaps we would be taken to a better place.

I matured some that night. My mind kept reviewing the Nazi's monologue. His English had been impeccable — far better than any of ours. And he knew his reasons for his war. He was older — possibly thirty; but our staff sergeant was twenty-eight and he had later dismissed the Nazi's comments with a thoughtless vulgarity.

It seemed we were against the very things the Nazi had said would be good. And I wondered how I could have become incarcerated in that despicable hole without having adopted personal convictions for helping fight the war.

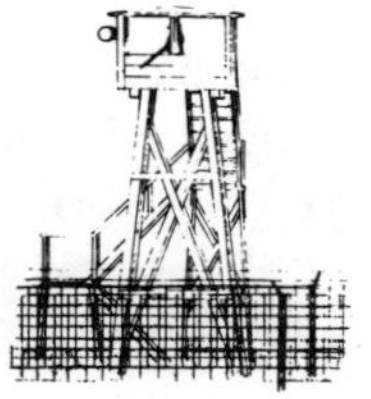

Chapter 2

Unrestricted

I had learned at the age of seven that there would never be another war. The moment was easy to remember because a visit to the cheesemaker was a momentous social outing for a young boy in the rural Midwest in 1931. According to family rules, I sat quietly next to my father unless asked a question, and my only word for the night was "seven" when our host asked how old I was.

The cheesemaker had not actually fought "in the front lines," but he had been in the World War, and he retold many of the frightening stories he had heard. I was intrigued.

He and my father agreed there could never be another war because they now had poison gas and airplanes. If battle lines were to form, each side would fly over the other, drop poison gas, and instantly wipe out the entire front. And if you couldn't fight a battle, you couldn't have a war. They also agreed that this confirmed the claim that the World War was "the war to end all wars."

After the visit, I was anxious to know more about that mysterious war that had been fought so that nothing like it could ever happen again. I remembered musical phrases about the war from a collection of phonograph records my parents had purchased years earlier along with a used Edison record player. There was no electricity on our farm, but there was no need; this was a mechanical player. Dates on the records' covers preceded the year 1920.

My older sister wound the crank and started the machine for me because I was considered too young to operate it. The tune that most intrigued me was a lilting march with occasional bugle flourishes in the background. The lyrics told of a valiant battle in which some of the fighting men apparently became prisoners of war. The last verse went:

So, within the prison cell,
We are waiting for the day,
That shall come to open wide the iron door.
And the hollow eye grows bright,
And the poor heart almost gay,
As we think of being home and brave once more.

My mother was pleased the first time the record was played — her oldest brother had fought in the front lines of that war. He was the uncle I had never met. He had married after the war and then lived near the Pacific coast.

My parents soon tired of my interest and suggested I listen to the records with religious hymns because that had been the main reason for getting the phonograph; the war had "ended long ago — thirteen years ago."

So we looked forward instead. We moved to a small town later where my father could retire to less arduous work, and where I could enter high school for a future with better opportunities. There were reports scattered over several years that someone called Hitler was gradually usurping control of all of Europe by annexing neighboring countries to Germany.

Then, on a quiet Sunday afternoon in December 1941, Americans were shocked by the most confusing news reports anyone could remember, and everyone was saying,

"Have you heard?"

"The Japs are bombing Pearl Harbor."

"No."

"What's Pearl Harbor?"

"That's our navy."

"Why? When did this start?"

"Our navy there is almost totally destroyed!"

"How could that happen? Where is that harbor?"

We crowded around a large piece of livingroom furniture called a radio and tried to interpret news reports.

By the following morning, everyone seemed furious; a commonly heard saying was, "We'll beat 'em before breakfast." Our high school principal summoned all students to the assembly hall to hear the nationally broadcast radio address of our country's President in which he referred to the "dastardly attack" on that date that would "live in infamy" in his request to the United States Congress for a declaration of war. In the next several days, radio evangelists quoted various scriptures to prove that the end of the world was imminent.

We had seldom listened to news before, but now we were concerned and curious. Reports from the war fronts were generally negative for the first months. They spoke of "withdrawals" to "predetermined positions in the rear" to "regroup men and equipment." All this while the nation "mobilized." News analysts compared efforts and effects with those of similar previous conflicts — and the Roman numeral "I" was appended to the title of the former world war.

Gasoline sales were restricted to four gallons per week for "unclassified" use in a personal automobile. This allowed about seventy miles of travel. There were car pools to almost everything. Sugar and meat ration coupons were controlled by local government boards.

Industries converted their consumer product activities to war production. Manufacture of automobiles was replaced by production of jeeps and "GI" (for Government Issue) trucks and half-tracks and tanks and reconnaissance cars. Buildings where these were made became known as "defense plants."

Silk stockings and rubber auto tires became unavailable, and many other items were scarce. Large-scale production for synthetic counterparts like nylon and neoprene were not yet developed, but parachutes and life rafts had to be supplied to air and sea forces.

It became patriotic to accept civilian shortages without complaining. Individual sentiments were absorbed into the feelings for the total cause. We sang, "Let's remember Pearl Harbor, As we did the Alamo," although many furtively queried, "What's the Alamo?" We commiserated when the verse of a new song described the adverse odds that were defeating a fighting unit — and we chorused along with the military chaplain who stepped in to help our troops annihilate the enemy while singing, "Praise the Lord, and pass the ammunition."

As the men went to "the service," the women went to work in defense plants. And the "home front" shared the glory. A blue "E" on a white triangular flag over a factory meant that that unit had exceeded a government-recommended level of efficiency in war production. The "tut-tut-tut . . ." of an orchestra's snare drum could make Rosie's riveting machine in an aircraft factory sound as effective as a machine gun:

> When they gave her the production 'E,'
> She was as proud as a girl could be.
> There's something true about,
> Red, white and blue about,
> Rosie (tut-tut-tut-tut-tut-tut-tut), the riveter.

A different tune with a similar purpose liltingly lauded "the woman behind the man behind the gun." And a comedian jokingly commended the draft board's discovery of a last hiding place for men still deferring their patriotism as he quipped it would no longer be possible to find a man behind the woman behind the man behind the gun.

The only way to get a visual impression of battle action was to watch "news reels" shown between feature films at movie theaters. Tense audiences quietly watched filmed attacks by our fighter planes spitting little spurts of fire from all wing guns. Spontaneous cheers and thunderous applause always followed the explosion of the enemy's equipment and vaporization of the fuel tanks into huge fire balls.

My preliminary medical exams and military registration forms were completed during the last months of high school so that I would be ready for official induction immediately after graduation.

* * *

Early in basic training in mid '43, under the sweltering Mississippi sun and humidity, I found that my bayonet wouldn't go through the suspended bag of sticks. The sergeants then explained I must yell "Kill" at the top of my lungs during a full-shouldered thrust as I ran the course. There were sixty thousand of us from all corners of the country. As "rookies," we consoled each other with leftover high school humor during breaks. We agreed we had just never had an urge to kill a bag of sticks before.

A few weeks later we were told that phosgene, mustard, lewisite, and chloropicrin were common poison gases in the world's arsenals — some blinded, some burned flesh. After instructions and practice with the gas mask and its carrying case, we were mildly tear-gassed, and we learned to yell "gas," hold our breath, yank the case open with one hand, and position the mask over the face with the other in about one second.

Our instructors informed us that we would carry the masks throughout the war but would probably never use them because more sophisticated methods of fighting had been developed since gas. I remembered that my father and the cheesemaker had agreed twelve years earlier that the availability of gas would preclude wars.

After basic training, I was sent to a radio communications school to develop one of the aptitudes discovered in tests at the induction center many weeks earlier.

While blizzards howled outside, ten thousand of us studied electronic theory and circuitry and practiced Morse code in wood-frame classrooms built on the plains of South Dakota for that purpose. We then fed coal to the three potbellied stoves in the barracks and slept while the other ten thousand students attended classes. Graduation assured a basis for proficiency in operation and maintenance of all communications equipment and systems used by the air forces in combat — all this in six months.

News reports on the progress of the war meanwhile continued to indicate that trends were turning toward our favor on all fronts because mobilization efforts were steadily improving.

A troop train bound for aerial gunnery school took me to the California-Mexico corner of Arizona. Here, we were told, we would learn to defend ourselves against any enemy attack, from any of the gun stations, in any aircraft type to which we might be assigned. An increasing need for air power had cut the time allotted for this from seven weeks to six; evening sessions had been added to meet the new schedule. We already knew the principles of aerial gunnery, they assured us; we just hadn't thought about them. We would merely need review, some numbers, and practice.

They were right. We started by watching movie films. One showed a boy tossing banded newspapers to front house doors while riding his bicycle on the sidewalk. Another showed running quarterbacks completing football passes to running receivers. These and others were analyzed with the conclusion that all projectiles follow the same laws of physics regardless of whether they're newspapers, footballs, or bullets.

Among Gila monsters and through searing desert sun or sandstorms, we fired shotguns at clay targets launched from trap and skeet houses and high towers. Our skills were further advanced as we stood on open trucks and shot at randomly directed targets while riding past launch stations.

By the third week we were firing 30 and 50 caliber machine guns from post mounts and from turrets. An initial target was a distant "bed sheet" mounted above a motorized carrier which sped through a trench in the desert; later there was a fuselage-size "sock" towed on a long cable behind an airplane.

Training culminated in battle-scarred B-17 bombers (the new ones went directly overseas). Student pilots in fighter planes from nearby airfields practiced "shooting us down" with movie cameras mounted on their guns while we practiced "shooting them down" with the cameras on our guns.

Our motivation improved in darkened rooms later when the exposed film strips compared efforts. We couldn't yell "Kill" now because we had to concentrate; with these weapons that were more humane than bayonets and more sophisticated than gas, the film showed the need for acuity: "Ya gotta get the bastard before he gets you."

Interspersed among shooting sessions were periods of associated training and testing. In a decompression chamber we learned we could retain alertness by wearing oxygen masks above ten thousand feet; and we observed the debilitating effects of anoxia by taking our turn without the mask at much higher altitudes.

Night vision capability was tested, as was depth perception, distance estimation, and color identification. We learned to disassemble and reassemble our guns in a limited time while blindfolded. We endured countless hours of sharpening our ability to identify all aircraft — ours, our allies', and our enemies'. And we finished the course in the reduced time schedule.

Prior to our shipping assignments, a sergeant in the exit process area audited test scores and performance levels. He pensively compared the results of my efforts with the requirements while he rocked a hand-stamp on an ink pad. Suddenly he slammed a large black word diagonally across my summary sheet, handed it over the desk to me, and pointed toward the next check station.

I concealed a swell of patriotic pride as I read "UNRESTRICTED" and settled against the wall to wait in line. Like the others, I was soon lost in personal thoughts. That was the most emphatic approval I had ever experienced. There had been no audience; "Pomp and Circumstances" had not been playing in the background; but my achievements had been soundly acknowledged. This meant I could fly day or night at any altitude in any aircraft.

I was a long way from home geographically, and — I realized somewhat whimsically — I was getting steadily farther from whatever "home" had been emotionally. Letters reporting which old friend said what to whom at the recent church meeting were almost meaningless now.

It had been a year since my graduation from high school. The speaker then had opened with a quote from Joshua 1:8:

> This book of the law shall not depart out of thy mouth; but thou shalt meditate therein day and night, that thou mayest observe to do according to all that is written therein: for then thou shalt make thy way prosperous, and then thou shalt have good success.

All the words and phrases the speaker had used were beautiful; but he had ignored the war. Red, white, and blue anchors stood on the chairs of three of the boys who had already left for the Navy; the rest were all scheduled to leave soon. How could he have ignored the war? Some of the villagers seemed to disapprove of our part in the war.

But my Uncle John from the west coast had recently introduced himself in a letter that was eloquent and also timely. He had gone back to school after his war, and then moved to Oregon later. He said that the twenty-six years since he had been in the trenches in France seemed a very short yesterday. He said my efforts were helping resolve the most crucial concerns that had ever confronted the world. He said he was sorry he couldn't say anything to help me, but apparently my battlefields would be in the sky, and he had no idea how they dug trenches among clouds.

Things he said had helped immensely. I hoped I could meet him in person very soon after my war was over. We would talk about causes and reasons and purposes.

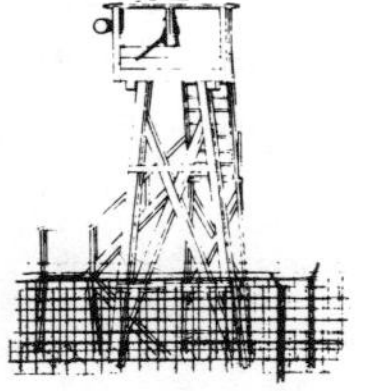

Chapter 3

Another Copilot?

We awoke to the high emotion of, "Did you hear? Have you heard? We're invading Europe!" While we packed our bags to leave gunnery school, radio broadcasts reviewed the progress of the invasion.

Various beaches on the northern coast of France were being assaulted by Allied troops and equipment from countless ships crossing the English Channel. Casualties were high, as expected, and initial resistance remained intense. But news analysts predicted cautiously that the mammoth military effort would be successful.

Establishment of a "western front" on the European continent had been anticipated for months, but only those in the highest military circles knew when, where, and how it would occur. Now that beginning, in June 1944, would be remembered by history as D-day.

In the elation of early successes there was even time for humor. Because kinds and quantities of military equipment shipped to England during the previous months had all been secret, newscasters could only report it as "massive amounts of tonnage"; much of it was now being transferred to the Continent, and they expressed relief that it had not sunk the British island.

As new graduates from a Service School, our personal thoughts soon turned to the next challenge: we were to report to a base in Nebraska for assignment to an Operational Training Center. That, however, was soon overshadowed by a surprise notice of a "delay en route" allowing seven days "at home" in the interim.

I found that anticipation of the homecoming while riding out two thousand miles on the train was the most enjoyable part of the leave. Once I reentered the village where my parents lived, I sensed an incredible sameness I hadn't expected, which seemed to alienate me. As servicemen, we had constantly seen changes everywhere, but the only difference here was a more depressed morale than when I left: these civilians didn't even show enthusiasm over the accomplishments of D-day.

Four years earlier, when Britain's Winston Churchill had told the world, "We shall fight on the beaches . . . fields . . . streets . . . we shall never surrender," he was admired, but the struggle was mostly "their problem." It had now been two and one-half years since we had reacted to the Japanese with, "We'll beat 'em before breakfast," and, if reminded that "there will always be an England," one wryly added, "as long as there's an America."

Shortages were more acute. I could converse with the "home folks" if I explained that photographic film was scarce because gunners were using it all in training. But I learned to avoid details that might not be considered decent, like the one about having to yell "Kill" while running the bayonet course. I was never sure of approval of the villagers.

Despite my misgivings, a conditioned respect for servicemen was evident. A small, red-bordered, rectangular white banner with a star at the center hung in the front window of every house with someone "off serving his country." Small-town newspapers listed all military transfers, promotions, accomplishments, and so on, of "their boys" as reported by each one's family.

Parents had become aware of a geography beyond that of their ethnic origins. My mother unfolded a United States map that she had purchased earlier at the "five and dime" to confirm locations of cities from which she had received my letters.

Unsettled feelings about the furlough as I rode the train to Nebraska made the uncertainty of the future a more welcome alternative.

I knew that the chances for assignment to the "heavies," Liberators or Flying Forts, were good. They were being applauded for precision bombing of synthetic oil refineries, aircraft factories, and other such targets, with minimum harm to civilians. And the military hierarchy seemed sure that intensification of such destruction would eventually debilitate the Third Reich's war machine.

After a week in Nebraska I emerged from another train at Davis-Monthan Field at Tucson, Arizona. Here I would join those who had trained in other specialties to become members of a flight crew. In three months we would finish the requirements together and be considered "combat ready."

Here, instead of a sameness, I sensed another difference. We were issued "Class A" passes. I had never heard the term. It meant we could come and go as we pleased while off duty. We would watch the schedules and complete our responsibilities, but there would be no more morning roll calls or midnight bed checks with hooded flashlights. In exchange for trustworthiness, we could expect to be trusted.

We would fly mornings, afternoons, and nights on a variety of "missions" — single plane flights at first and formation flights later — all simulating combat experience.

There seemed to be something comforting about hearing that the other men I would fly with would remain crew mates throughout the entire tour of duty overseas: that implied we would come back together. Initial meetings were brief; one was from Kansas, one from Alabama, and the others were from the East — we'd get to know each other later.

Rows of Liberator bombers stood gleaming in the sun as we approached the runways. Close-up looks while we checked numbers to find the plane we were to use for our first flight revealed they had been through countless hours of hard use.

The current day's sheet for encoding messages was in place on the tiny radio table behind the copilot's seat. There would be four of us here on the flight deck, "the best seats in the house." Vern was the flight engineer. He was on my left, directly behind the pilot. Gunners were in the nose, tail, and upper and lower turrets, and the navigator and bombardier were on the deck below us.

The half-hour of pre-flight checks passed quickly. I sat down to prepare a report I would transmit right after takeoff. Vern hoisted his shoulders through the upper hatch and called loudly, "Left aileron up. Right aileron down. Rudders left. Elevators down," as Sandy, our pilot, worked the controls.

Noise levels became deafening during revving to the high engine speeds required to read oil pressures and other measurements. After clearance from the control tower, we taxied into position near the end of the one-and-one-third-mile-long runway.

Sandy spread a wide hand across the four throttle levers and eased them steadily forward. Within seconds, the bouncing floor of the flight deck reminded me of a ride on the hayrack when my father had run the horses at full trot across a field to outrun a thunderstorm to the farm buildings. Vern slowly shouted, "Eighty, eighty-five, ninety, ninety-five . . . ," above the clatter as the blurring asphalt raced under the plane. We were "off with one helluva roar" as we had so often sung while marching to the tempo of "our song." Mesquite bushes and cactuses soon became a fuzzy green mottling in the vast brown of the desert.

I had to call the Second Air Force headquarters at Colorado Springs to tell them who we were, where we were, what we were doing, and why. I nervously rechecked the message, readjusted the earphones several times, and flexed my sending wrist over an open code key.

Colorado Springs was a vague name some six hundred miles to the northwest, according to the map. What if this assignment were a hoax? What if Colorado Springs didn't exist? I pretended this was a procedure exercise at radio school; Instructor Weber would then slide the little door open during the message to explain with a friendly smile what I was doing wrong.

Shortly after sending the call letters, a verification code from Colorado Springs came back and, at the end of the report, they casually confirmed with the Morse equivalent of, "Roger. Out."

I may have been a country bumpkin on a hayrack a few years earlier, but the Second Air Force headquarters had just acknowledged my transmission very respectfully. I felt a pleased smile coming on as I looked up to see the other three with smiles for their accomplishments already in place. When Sandy clicked into the intercom to learn the feelings of the others, the confidence of a seasoned crew seemed apparent: one jested, "We now have over six minutes of flying experience together behind us."

On later missions, we dropped "practice bombs" into white limed circles on the desert sand; small explosive charges in their noses puffed dust to show hits and misses. Every crew member's specialties were utilized in a variety of assignments. Vern and I manned the guns in the right and left waist windows when all positions needed tending.

On one of our first longer missions, we camera-bombed Bakersfield, California, without anyone there knowing. And we applauded our bombardier later when the developed film showed it had been successful.

Excessive wear in the engines of our war-weary planes provided unscheduled experience with emergencies. A smoking engine had to be shut off to prevent a fire, and uncompleted missions were rescheduled.

Sandy called a crew meeting after our first month as an operational unit. Everyone was there except our navigator; he, we learned, was the reason for the meeting. Had anyone befriended him? No. Had anyone tried? Yes, we all had. What did we know about him? Only that he had served a partial tour of duty in the Pacific Theater and had been reassigned here to complete his combat requirements. He had confirmed that much with a slight nod when someone tried to start a conversation; otherwise he never talked.

When he wasn't within hearing distance, we called him "the Blade" because he wore a hunting knife in a sheath on his belt as they did in the jungles. He was a large man; perhaps in his late twenties. We assumed he had a chip on his shoulder about something. Was he competent? As a navigator, yes; in some personal emergency, no one was sure.

When we met at the flight line for our next mission, Sandy introduced a new navigator. He was friendly and glad to be with us. A few weeks later we heard that Leebe, our former navigator, had been reassigned to another crew in their final week of training. Since he hadn't appeared to like us, we hoped this new arrangement might be better for all. No one suspected then that three months later and eight thousand miles away, we would hear the grisly end to his story.

One mission became more memorable than all other stateside experience.

We were in a six-plane formation at sixteen thousand feet nearing Alamogordo, New Mexico, when our number three engine started smoking. Soon after it was shut off, the number four engine failed; with no power on the starboard wing, we got immediate radio approval to turn back.

The initial comfort of being "on our way home" changed to anxiety when we learned we were steadily losing altitude with two ten-thousand-foot mountain ranges yet to cross. A small gasoline engine, normally called a "putt putt" from the sound it made, could have supplanted the electrical power lost with the first engine. When Vern reported it inoperable we promptly shut down everything electrical that was not essential to remaining airborne.

The long wall of mountains on the horizon ahead prompted Ronnie, our copilot, to wonder if there could be an alternate landing site. Sandy shrugged and waved a hand disparagingly toward the endless desolation below.

"There it is! That's got to be a landing strip," Ronnie suddenly shouted as he jabbed an index finger excitedly against his side window. A short, thin, light line could be seen in the desert's dark brown, five miles to the right. "You cannot, you will not, find a pass through those mountains," Ronnie insisted. "Anyhow, they're half an hour away and we're down to nine thousand feet and still dropping," he added as he pointed to the altimeter.

After several glances, Sandy said, "We'll take it." We would land in two minutes. From our distance, there appeared to be no control tower or other buildings. I fired two red distress flares through the cabin-roof orifice to tell anyone at the strip that we were on an emergency landing approach.

When Sandy called for fifteen degrees of flaps to help control the descent, it became shockingly apparent that the flaps didn't work; they were normally driven by the hydraulic system, which had quit with the number three engine. To compensate for the half-minute lost, Ronnie's right hand went into violent pumping of the manual alternate, a handle beside the copilot's seat.

Sandy then yelled, "Wheels," realizing that they wouldn't come down for the same reason. Vern dove down to the bomb bay door behind us and bellowed, "Help!" into the nose area below. Two large cranks on the wall just inside the bomb bay would slowly bring the landing gear down manually. Fifteen turns lowered the wheel and fifteen more locked it into landing position. Vern was already cranking one when the bombardier moved back to work the other.

At nine hundred feet, Sandy realized he would have to maintain altitude and circle the landing strip while waiting for flaps and wheels. When he couldn't initiate a turn to the left without power on the right wing, he was anxious to make the alternate move. Like any good pilot, he later called his next impulse a mistake; instead of "fish-tailing" in a level turn to the right, he banked.

I have relived the following sequence in nightmare form at various times since. The bank went directly into a sideslip and, in a sickening drop, we fell sideways toward the desert only six seconds out of my window.

Sandy and Ronnie each shrieked the other's name as they twisted their control wheel and rammed it forward. This put the plane into a nose dive to regain speed and restore flight characteristics. Still shrieking, they then strained to nearly supine positions to force the left rudder pedals with both feet, and pulled the controls back to bring the nose up.

At over one hundred miles per hour, we rolled into the desert almost horizontally in a deafening cacophony of booms, crashes, and rasping and grinding sounds. I bounced like a ping-pong ball between the radio table, ceiling, wall, and copilot's seat, as sand and gravel hailed against my window and cactuses and mesquite bushes catapulted into the air and tumbled over the wing.

Suddenly, there was a gigantic lurch, the nose portion skewed to the right and we bounced sideways toward the left. Retrospectively, I counted four large bounces followed by a series of smaller ones.

I was hoisting myself through the top hatch with a half-dozen hands pushing up on my feet and legs as we shuddered to a stop. The nose and right wing-tip had furrowed into the sand. High and to my right, bodies were leaping from the right-waist window as I ran down the wing with someone close behind.

We raced together through the sparse desert brush to a spot sixty yards from the wreckage. There we turned and stared, shivering, too bewildered to speak. All ten of us had been sure there would be an explosion and a huge fireball. But she just lay there — with the left wing and the tail section pointed toward the sky — as if in disrespect for man's efforts to try to make her fly. The utter quiet was hard to comprehend.

We all had scuffs, bumps, bruises, and tender spots. There were a couple of rips in clothing. But there was no flowing blood, and there were no broken bones.

For one moment we looked at each other and giggled like grade-school girls, and then we stared at the plane again.

Sandy finally broke a scary silence with, "I surely couldn't have turned her out of that slip without you, Ronnie." Ronnie pondered, shook his head and said, "I can't believe we pulled her out of that dive, even with the two of us." And then, after another silence, someone else said, "Maybe we had another copilot up there pulling for us."

We had just begun to compare the confusing anomalies of surviving a crash-landing when three black horses galloped up. Their riders, two young men and a lady, were dressed in dude cowboy garb. Out for a ride, they had seen our erratic dive and the half-mile-long sand cloud rise out of the desert. From the "endless thunder" following the cloud, they thought we'd be much closer than the "couple miles" they had ridden to find us. When convinced we were well, they told us our crash path crossed a graded country road a short walk back.

A frightened middle-aged man then came panting through the brush. He hadn't expected to find survivors. He owned a ranch house a mile from there; he had also assumed it would be a short run to the wreckage.

Before long a car stopped on the road and the occupants came running. After another car stopped, there were enough spectators to exchange stories among themselves while we analyzed details.

We strolled back along the landing path our plane had gouged and found the right landing gear among bushes near the road. Some distance away, there was a large section of a bomb bay door.

The gigantic lurch had occurred as we bounced over the road. Both wheels were then down, but the gear that had torn loose was not yet locked in place. The bombardier had clung to the wheel's crank handle when the catwalk slipped out from under his feet as the plane's belly hit the ground.

The bomb bay door had shot through the waist partition and out through the side of the plane; it caught the sleeve of Vern's fleece-lined leather jacket at the wrist and tore out a narrow triangle to the shoulder, but left only scuff marks on his arm.

We learned there were no buildings at the air strip we had intended to use because it was under construction. It was a military installation, it was being graded, and no one could have survived a collision with the large bulldozer working at the center.

Willcox, a town of twelve hundred people, was five miles away and approximately eighty miles from Tucson. Sandy elected to stay with the plane, Ronnie went to telephone the base from Willcox, and the rest of us accepted the rancher's invitation for lunch at his home.

We returned an hour later to find a mile of cars parked along the little road, three military police ambling about inside a roped area around our plane, and a crowd of three hundred spectators discussing what it must have felt like to dive into the crash site. The MP's obdurately followed their orders and refused us entry to retrieve personal items. Two "recon cars" from Davis-Monthan were on the way out to pick us up.

Our inexorable commanding officer, known only as "the Major" around the airbase, piloted a light single-engine plane; he flew out to personally view the scene. He was circling our wreckage like a vulture when we left twenty minutes later.

Our drivers were WAC's. They professed to know nothing about the reaction to news of the crash back at the base. They took us directly to a "detention" area, where we were directed into separate rooms and given a pad and pencil and a half-hour to describe what had happened and what our personal role had been in attempting to prevent or correct problems.

After individual oral reviews, we were released with orders not to dicuss the reports with anyone, and to return in the morning. We had assumed we might be heroes among our peers for having survived; now we wondered if we were some kind of criminals.

We learned the following morning that the afternoon flight schedules had been canceled and all flying personnel were to assemble in the band shell at 1300 hours. It became apparent there that the Major, in addition to being CO and his own pilot, was also an aspiring orator.

He started quietly explaining to the audience of several hundred that the Air Force courses were not like those in high school because these could not be repeated if the student forgot what he had learned. He gibed that he hadn't realized how many simple basic essentials for successful flight, like common perception, were being casually ignored. He read a line from one of our reports saying the tail gunner had turned his master turret switch off; inspectors found it on.

He reported that the flight engineer had written that he couldn't start the putt putt; the reason, given during the oral review, was that he couldn't find the starting rope. By now the Major was becoming vehement. "And why the hell did they make the GI belt like they did?" he shouted as he stripped his belt through its loops.

"Remember?" he bellowed while the belt dangled like a snake at arm's length. "They told us back in basic training that our trousers were fitted so that we didn't really need a belt, but the loops were a handy place to carry such a versatile tool. Remember? It serves as a tourniquet if you're injured, a sling if you've got a lot to carry, a tether if you've got to lead or drag something, a fetter if you have to tie your prisoner's hands behind his back. Remember?

"It will also start a putt putt as easily as the rope that should have been there," he grumbled as he fed his belt back through its loops.

He concluded finally with the order that all crew members explain all their responsibilities to all other crew members, demonstrate how to handle emergencies, discuss how to cover for each other, and so on.

We left chagrined, but consoling peers reminded us that the Major had never implied our crash could have been averted with the increased diligence he recommended.

Vern refused to discuss anything. Suddenly, he disappeared. He reappeared the next day to pick up toilet articles and a change of clothes. He said he was temporarily billeted at the detention area, he would probably be shipped over to some never-never outpost to hose down airplanes until long after the "duration plus," but he felt he'd have half a chance of staying alive — he had decided to quit flying.

"You can't," we chorused.

"I can if I get airsick," he retorted.

"But you don't get airsick."

"I get airsick," he grinned.

"They'll courtmartial you."

"Not if I prove I'm airsick while flying with two medics."

Obviously, he had considered the details.

He walked in three days later appearing pale and disheveled and said, "I'm shipping," as he threw things into his bag.

"What do you mean, 'Shipping'?"

"Shipping out."

"Did you take your airsickness test?"

"Just finished," he said, thumbing toward the door.

"Did you get sick?" someone asked.

"I puked all over that airplane," he grinned. Then he convulsed and giggled through, "I even puked on one of the meds watching me."

"What did you take to get sick?"

"Look, I'm not supposed to talk to you guys. The MP in the jeep out front gave me exactly sixty seconds to pick up my junk and get back out."

He slung his bag over his shoulder and, without looking, waved a backhand over the other shoulder as he went through the door and disappeared again — this time, forever.

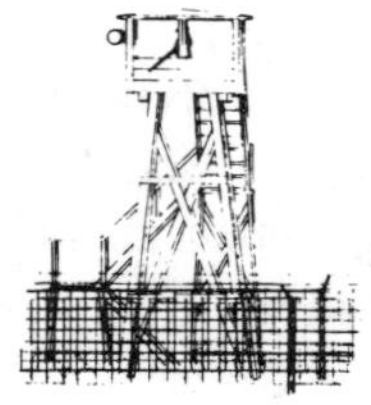

Chapter 4

Joe Ees Son Off O Beech

Our new flight engineer was from Idaho. We called him Elk. He had been nicknamed that by members of a previous crew and said he rather enjoyed it.

After completing the requirements for Operational Training (OT), we received shipping orders to a staging area at Topeka, Kansas, from where we would travel to an unknown port of embarkation and on to an unknown combat assignment. The orders again included a one-week delay en route for an interim visit at "home."

This time I would not be disappointed because I would know what to expect and that a week was too short to preplan any socializing. This time I would bid goodbye to people without using that word. And this time I would take a fond last look at certain places and hope I might look at them, perhaps from another aspect, on some future date.

I rode a bus from my parents' house to the nearest city, where the village youths went to seek better entertainment and the elders went to shop for better bargains. I took a seat near the tiny entertainment stage at the Two Hearts Cafe in the evening, hoping to review fond memories of past visits. The men at the bar, however, were outshouting all reminiscent moods with arguments of what had to be done to the "damn Germans" and the "damn Japs" in order to end the "damn war."

The sweet and romantic melodies of the guitarist seemed to go unnoticed — and he appeared to try to ignore the war talk. After pensively picking through the "Isle Of Capri," he started singing softly:

> T'was on a pile of debris that I found her,
> Out behind the old brewery,

> There were boxes, cans ’n bottles strewn around her,
> When we met on that pile of debris.

He nodded and warmly returned my smile, apparently grateful that one person out there had heard his efforts to entertain.

Near the end of the furlough my mother wondered if I might now teach in a radio school as another mother’s son in the village was doing. I retorted I was being assigned to a combat unit and would go overseas with my crew — I knew she had known that but wasn’t accepting it.

I left home again wondering if anyone there approved of the trend my training had taken. Disturbed by my doubts, I listened instead to a current song that said, “There’s something about a soldier that is fine, fine, fine.”

After a week in Topeka we boarded a troop train bound toward a location known only as the POE. During the day, it was obvious we were headed eastward. At night, when the metallic rhythm of the wheels on the rails slowed and body mass sagged toward the outside on the long curves, we knew we were winding through mountains — some part of the Allegheny range. Late in the morning, we detrained inside a fenced area called Camp Patrick Henry.

We were briefed in large groups in a lecture hall by an appropriately humorous security officer. He told us that the local city was Newport News, Virginia, near Norfolk, but that we would see it only from GI trucks as we rode past to board ships in the next few days.

He explained that the absence of telephone booths was intended. We would be given an APO number to use as an address, and only the American post office would know how to find us. We were to write nothing about where we were, had been, or thought we would be going; similarly, nothing about work or other activities that could be interpreted militarily or geographically.

Everything would be reviewed by a censor who followed the rule, “If in doubt, cut it out.” He begged that we not write, “After I mailed my last letter, I met Virginia Newport, but she didn’t have any news,” because they were very weary of cutting that.

He said he called one soldier in and asked, “What makes you think you’re going to Italy?” When the man seemed bewildered, he showed him his envelope addressed to a “Miss” somebody; “ITALY” was boldly printed across the back. The embarrassed soldier explained that that was a romantic acronym. “We’ve always used it. It means, ‘I treasure and love you.’ ”

Embarkation was new and different. We transferred from the GI truck to a ferryboat for the ride to our ship. While similar loadings appeared to be progressing everywhere around us, we boarded the *David G. Farragut*. An eighty-two-ship convoy was being assembled. The waters of the Atlantic were no longer considered “infested” with German U-boats now, in late 1944, but the adage about strength in numbers was still being heeded.

Our ship was manned by Merchant Marine personnel accustomed to answering questions like the ones we asked. We were aboard a 450-foot "Liberty ship," smaller than many but otherwise typical of those used to transport troops. Crews tending the guns mounted on the periphery of the deck were from the Navy. If our ship's 350-man cargo was typical, thirty thousand newly trained fighting men would be going overseas at this time. However, some of the vessels carried supplies and equipment.

As we steamed from the lower end of Chesapeake Bay, our convoy formed into an elongated oval with the leading ships appearing to be ten miles ahead to the east-southeast. From the trailing end of the formation, we were the last to press against the rear railings to strain our eyesight and question whether that thin line on the horizon was a last view of our homeland — or was now just part of our imagination.

There were thirty-five Air Force navigators among the aircrew personnel on our ship. Curiosity, practice, and boredom were the reasons given for many of them to bring out their sextants to confirm our location. Destination remained a military secret, but we always knew our position and direction.

After a week at sea we were one-third of the way to Africa when our course changed to due east. This ended concern of whether we might go around the Cape of Good Hope to the Pacific or the China-Burma-India area. The speed of the convoy, limited by the slowest ship, remained a steady nine knots. Each wave that broke against the bow looked like the preceding one; impatience grew but eventually stabilized.

A common pastime for players and a large group of spectators was a raucous game of craps promoted daily by a Merchant Marine kitchen helper. The promoter was considered more merchant than marine when he revealed to annoyed losers after the voyage that his two-thousand-dollar winnings were about average for a one-way trip. "A hell of a lot of 'em," was his best guess for the number of trips he had made since the war started.

Everyone became very fond of the smiling face and cheerful personality of Lieutenant Miligan. He was in charge of clicking the hand counter as diners queued into the mess line, and although he had counted each of us eighty-seven times before debarkation he seemed always to find a new and pleasant greeting. Few could have believed that he would be barely recognizable through scarred features when some of us would meet him again behind enemy lines several weeks later.

At the end of the second week our course changed to east-northeast — directly toward the Strait of Gibraltar. By now, time had lulled us into a psychologically unreal sort of existence. Conversational pastimes seemed to evolve around fantasies for things to do after the war.

Then suddenly, early one morning in the third week, the cheer of "Land!" reverberating about the ship brought reality back into our lives. The line on the horizon off our starboard side was confirmed as the northwest coast of Africa. There was a childish comfort about being "near somewhere" and the good feeling that it looked "just like home" from that distance.

We were surprised the next day when our convoy started veering northward "toward England." We were surprised again twenty minutes later when, after the first thirty ships took that turn, the rest of us continued on our former course.

The immensity of the Rock of Gibraltar was impressive; as we glided past in the strait, it seemed close enough to touch.

After a few days in the Mediterranean, the coast of Africa faded to leave us "at sea" with a raging autumn gale. The violence of the storm increased until gigantic waves broke onto the deck, and all ships faced into the wind to minimize roll in favor of the safer pitch position. A day's progress was lost as the convoy treaded water and passengers stayed below deck to worry, while the ship's screw growled whenever the stern rocked out of the water.

The Navy initiated a gunnery practice session after we had passed the island of Sardinia. The 20-millimeter guns along the edge of the deck started chugging away at the large balloons rising on a north breeze; shells were then pitched like cordwood to the "three incher" on the bow for surviving balloons; and finally, the "five incher" on the stern rocked us while attempting to pop those still drifting toward Africa.

It was a grand show. Although a basic respect between branches of the service always ran deep and true, this was an opportune time for rivalry gibes — we told the sailors they were lucky to be in the Navy because we would have been courtmartialed for that many misses.

While the lead ships continued eastward, probably toward the Suez Canal, our third of the original convoy turned north to take us up the eastern shore of Sicily. Anchors were dropped in the harbor at Augusta within view of the magnificent pastel reflections of Mt. Etna.

We were apparently ahead of somebody's schedule, because we waited two days before steaming through the Strait of Messina to marvel at how the little clusters of houses clung to the steep hillsides just above water level on the west shore of Italy..

Dusk fell rapidly as we slid quietly toward the harbor at Naples. Then there was a sudden rush toward the port-side rail as word of a significant passing spread about the deck: "The Isle of Capri! That's her. There she is. That's the Isle of Capri!" She rose steeply from the water. The hillside facing us appeared wooded in the near dark. She would have been just another island except that someone had put romantic words to music.

Now everyone fell silent amid his own thoughts. I remembered the Two Hearts Cafe near home, and I questioned why I had never wondered where this island was, or if it were real.

Only two hundred miles from the battle lines north of Rome, our anchor dropped in almost total darkness. "Blackouts" here were far darker than those we spoke of back in the States.

Sunrise brought a beautiful view of Mt. Vesuvius, distant rolling hills, and aged stone buildings in Naples, just as the pictures in our world-history books had protrayed them a few years earlier. The local scene, however, showed the world's history had not been beautiful in recent years. Superstructures of sunken ships jutted from the water randomly about the harbor: people of the world were still far too busy sinking other ships to consider cleaning up the mess they were leaving.

After twenty-nine days of compensating for wave motion, the concrete dock seemed cruelly stable and solid to our first steps. Waiting GI trucks took us speeding down deserted streets and over dusty roads through old vineyards to a tent city eleven miles east of Naples. The tent for our crew's six enlisted men overlooked a trampled meadow.

This deployment camp had been here most of the time since Allied forces first occupied the area a year earlier, and local children had learned how to watch for new troop shipments. They were soon approaching our fence with extended hands and a clamor of "moon-yea Eye-tal-yon?" They held out Italian coins that had become useless except for selling to gullible American souvenir collectors.

The children knew that this first day would be the most lucrative for them; they knew the value of our money and how to dicker for the most of it, and they knew how to watch for the white helmets worn by our guards, who inevitably got to all areas of the camp. At the sight of a helmet, the children scampered across the field like rabbits as bullets from the guard's service pistol kicked up little spurts of dirt from the ground around them. (The guard force boasted a clean record of never having hit any of the children, even though the little spurts of dirt had to be dangerously close to discourage their infiltration of our camp for rampant thievery.)

Bright November days warmed to t-shirt comfort. We played cards on the canvas cots with the tent sides open to the sun while awaiting further move-orders. But our clothing and blankets were inadequate for tent life during long night hours when bone-chilling cold settled onto the Mediterranean peninsula.

A message posted in the information area indicated that newly arrived air crews would probably not move for several days; it concluded with, "Read all notices on this bulletin board once daily for further orders." These were welcome instructions. We were free to be tourists in the surrounding area.

The upper turret gunner and I agreed to see the local town of Caserta together. Other than American transport vehicles, there were only occasional horse-drawn carts; hitchhiking on GI trucks was "the only way to travel."

The city had not been physically damaged by war because it was of no military significance. Compared to American cities we knew, there seemed to be very little activity in the streets. A few young children played improvised games. Older men begged; when they thought it worth the effort, they dropped their hands from a praying position to open palms while plaintively monotoning, "Multi bambino, no moolah."

There appeared to be little spirit to try to venture beyond mere existence. The succession of stone buildings lining the streets had apparently never borne signs to advertise goods or services, or even to distinguish between business and residential entrances. Shops were few and small and contained only souvenirs and curios handmade from paper, wood, or soft metals like copper, lead, or tin.

A black-haired, dark-eyed, attractive young lady approached to offer assistance as we entered one of the stores. After we explained that we were new to the country and mostly curious, she assured us with flawed but delightfully understandable English that we were most welcome to browse because the presence of American soldiers always charmed Italian ladies.

She was amused when we questioned whether Italian ladies had similarly flattered German soldiers while they were present in recent years; and she laughingly confirmed that they certainly had. We agreed they probably preferred their own countrymen, but none dared to be that honest during current military occupations.

At a restaurant two violinists interrupted their medley to become fiddlers and swing into the then popular American ditty "Rum and Coca Cola," to honor our entry. They too used humorously accented English and stressed lines like:

> . . . Native girls all dance and smile.
> They wear grass skirts, but that's okay,
> 'Cause Yankee like to hit the hay-ay.

The food was as bad as the hypocritical welcome.

I took my next day's trip alone. The truck-driver dropped me on a corner in Naples that he said was "as good as any." I first stood in excited awe for several minutes gazing at the many massive stone buildings. Because international travel was affordable only to the wealthy, I felt very fortunate. I had decided to pretend there was no war for these first hours, and that I was privileged to experience here what I had assumed a short three years earlier I would see only as pictures in my geography book.

I noticed a small boy, who had been watching me intently, turn toward me as I started on a walk. He appeared to be a friendly seven-year-old. He extended his palm with three coins and politely questioned, "Moon-yea Eye-tal-yon?" I stooped to inspect his wares, and an impish smile spread across his face, apparently in appreciation of my interest. I was about to explain that his coins were too common to be salable here when he expectantly whispered, "Sleep weeth my seester, Joe?"

I snapped erect and swirled back onto the course I had been following. He was not an imp; he was a pimp! His coins were decoys.

"Jeest like virgin, Joe," he called. He was following me.

"Joe," he shouted angrily, "Seester ees jeest like virgin." He was falling behind.

"Joe ees son off o beech," he muttered. He had given up.

There were others like him in other blocks, but they were easy to avoid now that I knew the approach. I had heard about Maria Gonorrhea and Phyllis Syphilis — I had seen the Service films. I had even heard most of the barracks stories about all the things that "Dirty Gertie from Bizerte" could do. But now I was amazed at how much more this seven-year-old boy in Naples knew about the sordid aspects of war than I had known.

When I was seven, the cheesemaker had told us about the gory side of war. His stories had originated on "battlefields" which sounded like hayfields or cornfields on our farm — areas that men selected to do bloody things to each other. I hadn't thought of the effects that battlefield activities had on the contiguous society.

The reasons for things I had been observing in this country were now becoming more clear. These people, whose leader had joined their efforts to Hitler's, had seen their armies losing a fight for dominance. And they were losing faith in their government and each other and their monetary system.

Our money was labeled "Allied Military Currency" but marked in *lire* coordinated with the Italian denominations. Most locals considered it ultimately safer. So, although they hated us for overrunning their land, they tried to flatter us like the clerk in the curio store, or entertain us like the fiddlers in the restaurant, or entice us like this seven-year-old.

This boy's schooling couldn't start until his elders could reorganize schools, but he obviously had already learned from sidewalk economics that he wouldn't get a commission if he hadn't made a sale.

On a corner a few blocks down the street, I found a tour-group of American GI's being formed by an enterprising Italian guide. For a small fee in "moonyea Amerikon," he walked the few percent who were interested in this sort of thing to local significant buildings while summarizing bits of their history. Although we sometimes doubted his veracity, details were often fascinating.

Other natives guided similar tours in different areas. Guides characteristically felt that we were most interested in the sensuous facets of their stories, so they told how various famous persons' sexual pursuits had changed the course of history.

Numerous sidewalk vendors interjected offerings of "feelthy peek-chures" and "feelthy" statuettes. I knew many years later that someone who had become a cartoonist had gotten the same impression I had, because I opened a magazine to a cartoon showing a sleazy character in a wide-brimmed hat and an ill-fitting cloak extending a hand while asking, "You like buy feelthy Easter eggs?"

I spent the next few days visiting other sites in the area. I went to Pompeii, the resort city for wealthy Romans until it was cataclysmally inundated by wet ashes and cinders from Mt. Vesuvius in 79 AD. In the parts that had since been excavated, we saw narrow stone streets where the ruts, worn several inches deep by chariot wheels, had served as that then-beautiful city's sewerage system.

Because of initial comparison to American troop trains, a short trip on an Italian train seemed like a novelty ride at a country fair. The sensation was due partly to the smaller size, and partly to lights that burned brightly at higher speeds but faded to total darkness as we slowed to stops in tunnels.

I saw a partially excavated, recessed amphitheater where, our guide informed, wealthy Romans had no doubt cheered as lions mauled and devoured Christians on Sunday afternoons nineteen hundred years earlier.

And then a notice on our bulletin board read, "Members of all crews listed below will assemble at 0700 hours. . . ." Someday I would ponder the meaning of things I had seen, but now it was time to get on with the job of trying to finish the war.

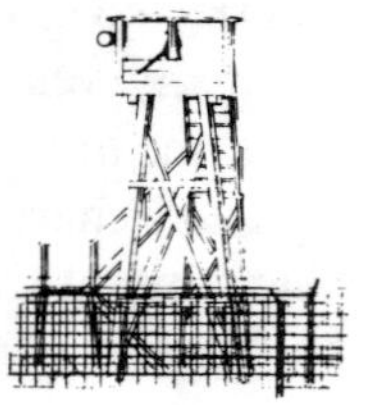

Chapter 5

16 December 1944

An eighty-mile ride from Caserta took us to our new base near Cerignola, inland from the Adriatic Sea and just below the spur of the boot of Italy. Combat units of the Fifteenth Air Force were spread over much of this area.

Accomplishments of the bomb group we were joining were summarized during a short introductory welcome. And we were encouraged to adopt an esprit de corps because our contributions would "soon add to those statistics."

Many airfields in this area, abandoned earlier by fleeing Germans, had since been adapted for our use. We occupied what had apparently once been a magnificent Italian farm. The main house and servant quarters, after rough additions and modifications, served as a mess hall and administration building. A converted shed or granary was now a canteen and service club combination.

Our troops were housed in existing outbuildings and various four- or six-man fieldstone "huts" constructed by the crews that had first lived in them.

Eighteen of us, the enlisted men of three crews that had lived together in Operational Training at Tucson, were assigned to a wing of one of two large U-shaped barns. As the early December weather froze the nights, we hurried to convert a sixty-gallon drum into a gasoline space heater, and to complete myriad modifications to make the barn "our home" for thirty-five missions over the next several months.

Our efforts were soon interrupted for a practice flight to sharpen skills that had atrophied in the weeks of disuse. A short truck ride over the "back eighty" took us to Quonset huts near the flight line for parachutes, ammunition, and other equipment. Patches and water puddles on the runway reminded us that asphalting equipment was not as available here as in the States. Soon after takeoff, we got a first look at the Adriatic. And we hedge-hopped to strafe designated ground targets on local side hills.

First meals in the mess hall proved it was enlightening to listen well to discussions among others at our table and those around us. These men were veterans. Whether they had flown one mission or thirty-four, they were mutually respectful of the grim business of surviving reverberating black clouds of flak over the targets and fighter attacks along the way.

There was no pride of individual accomplishment here, or boasting about comparative achievements. And there was no jesting about those who hadn't been up yet because everyone knew that would happen tomorrow or a day after. There was no overt elation by those who had completed thirty-four missions, because everyone remembered "the one who got his on his thirty-fifth." Discussions were not intended to impress or intrigue; experiences were shared only because better understanding of techniques and tactics could improve the odds for survival.

Hartfield, our tail gunner, and I were eavesdropping on a breakfast discussion about possible ways to evade the White Guards. These were outlaws who remained sympathetic with Hitler's efforts. They were scattered in the mountains of northern Italy, and they attempted to dispirit air crews who suffered the misfortune of having to bail out of disabled aircraft on their return from targets to the north. Tactics of the White Guards followed a pattern of a gruesome execution of half the crew members, generally the officers, while the others watched, and then sending the survivors back with the stories and "dog tags" of the victims.

Suddenly, Hart asked, "Did you hear the name Dave Leebe?"

"Yes, I was about to ask you the same question," I answered. I slid over and told the man that we had had a navigator with the name Dave Leebe in OT at Tucson, and asked if he had just mentioned that name.

"Yeah, he's dead."

"Did this one wear a hunting knife in a sheath on his belt like some do in the Pacific?"

"Yeah, all the time."

"The one we knew was transferred to a crew that left about a month before we did. If this is the same one, this must have been quite recent."

"Yeah, it happened a couple weeks ago, and they were on like about their second mission."

"Was he from . . .? Had he been . . .? Did he have . . .?" There was no need to doubt the identity — everything checked. "How did he die?"

"On a meat hook."

"What do you mean, 'a meat hook'?"

The man crooked his middle finger and said, "Just a big metal hook with a hand-loop on it like a butcher uses to drag a carcass on a cutting table. The White Guards got him."

"But, how. . .?"

He interrrupted with an answer to a different question than I had intended. He placed a thumbnail against his Adam's apple and rammed it toward his chin as he said, "Just like that; right through their tongues and the roofs of their mouths — five of them in a row. Then they hoisted the hand loops over a row of hooks and let them kick and gurgle with their hands tied behind their backs for as long as it lasted while the rest of the crew watched."

After an awkward silence, I asked, "Are the other crew members here?"

"No. They were sick. They got back a few days after their ordeal, but they were only here for part of a day. They probably got taken to some shrink hospital, and then back to the States. They'll wind up as instructors or clerks or drill sergeants or something."

The "locals," also known as "Eye-ties," who worked in our mess hall communicated in only three words: "Fin-ney, fin-ney," if we asked for more of any food variety that was rationed, and, "No capeesh, no capeesh," if we talked about anything else. The one at the scrape table altered the sequence when he objected to our departure with an excited, "No fin-ney, no fin-ney," as Hart and I put our trays down.

We knew he was trying to tell us we hadn't finished our food, and we realized that his conscience was telling us we should eat all we had taken. But I didn't realize until we were halfway back to our quarters that I had yelled in his face, "We got sick. You eat it. Okay?"

Our space heater was complete and working well, but there had not yet been time to do any of the things to make the barn feel homey when a first mission was assigned to one of our three crews. They were listed on the flight board after the evening meal along with all others in the squadron who would fly combat the next day.

We were very quiet in the early evening, respecting their attempts to sleep, to restore whatever extra acuity they might need.

They seemed withdrawn when they returned the following evening. Flak over the target had been rough; they had holes in their plane, but they didn't want to talk about it. It had been a long mission — and a long session in postmission interrogation. They felt it might be better if we discussed feelings later, maybe after we had all completed some combat missions. We wondered if they'd ever again have the optimistic, cheerful, normal personalities we had known.

The second crew found their assignment listed after another day. And again, we pretended to be busy while we were quietly concerned about their welfare.

No one had yet dared to mention that they were two hours later than the normal return time the next evening when, suddenly, one of their gunners came panting out of the night's darkness with much of his parachute gathered over an arm and the rest dragging behind. He was frightened. He demanded to know where the rest of his crew was.

Once convinced that he was the first we had seen, he hastily explained that they had been hit over the target but couldn't assess the effect of the damages. They had flown directly back and then continued circling to test the controls and expend fuel. Still unsure of whether or not the landing gear would operate, the pilot decided to bring the plane in alone after the crew had bailed out.

A messenger from the flight line informed us later that the pilot was not injured despite further damage during landing. The others dragged their chutes in from various directions during the next two hours.

The following day our crew attended a meeting to learn about conditions in areas we would eventually fly over. Since most targets of the Fifteenth Air Force were toward eastern Europe, we would commonly cross the Adriatic and then Yugoslavia; attitudes toward downed airmen there were reportedly improving daily. Chetniks and Partisans, they told us, were the factions vying for recognition in the Yugoslavian government; the Partisans were gaining control, and they were on our side.

"If you must abandon ship over Yugo," they advised, "get with the Partisans and you'll be returned here comfortably, smoking American cigarettes all the way." This session concluded precombat requirements, they said, but did not necessarily mean we would fly in the next few days.

On return from the evening meal, I scanned the flight board, casually wondering whom I might know among those assigned a mission for the following day. At midpoint on the list, I stopped, reread, shook off a shiver, and reread again — it was our crew.

A dim circle of light reflected from a white paper on a clipboard. A man kneeling beside my cot was quietly asking if this name on his list was mine, if the serial number was correct and if I knew this was the sixteenth of December. I muttered confirmations. I snapped erect when he asked if I remembered I had been assigned to fly a mission today. Of course, I remembered!

I was momentarily annoyed that I had been unable to sleep until the previous hour, but there was no time to fret. We stumbled through the icy darkness to the mess hall. Then we waited for the truck and shivered over the bumpy trail to the flight line.

The door to the large briefing room opened continuously as airmen hurried in from all directions to identify themselves as they passed the checkoff roster. After the door was locked, one of the officers on stage announced that all were now present or accounted for. He then whipped open a curtain to expose a large wall map of central Europe, and a dismal groan from the crowd slowly became audible.

A strand of green yarn spanned the map from bottom to top. Starting at our base, it crossed the Adriatic, skirted Italy over northern Yugoslavia, and extended to the northwest corner of Czechoslovakia. Another rookie behind me whispered to the man next to him, "What's wrong with that?"

"The distance," the man snapped, "Every trip gets longer. It'll take all day to get there. That's only a hundred miles south of Berlin!"

Quiet fell across the crowd as the initial briefing officer cleared his throat to say, "First of all, this mission is probably not going to be as bad as many of you seem to think." He agreed it would be a long ride but assured us it was well planned and strategically important. Because gas load had to be substituted for bomb load, each plane would carry only six of the five-hundred-pound bombs. As we would see at the rendezvous, however, the number of planes had been increased to compensate.

Our target was one of the Third Reich's dwindling number of large synthetic oil producers, known to us as the Brux refinery. Our lead plane would reach the "Initial Point" east of the target at 1220 hours, and demolition of the refinery would begin at 1236 hours. The altitude of the bomb run would be 25,500 feet, just under the 26,000-foot ceiling for the currently used models of the B-24.

A meteorologist discussed weather conditions anticipated for our route, and another officer reviewed expected enemy defenses. Fighter plane activity should be nil, he said, because the Germans were conserving their remaining gas and oil to support their western front. Intense flak on the bomb run was likely, however, because German Intelligence seemed to be increasingly able to anticipate our strikes, their antiaircraft guns were very mobile, and their accuracy and effectiveness continued to improve.

A shorter string of red yarn to an alternate target in Austria was no longer needed. Minor industrial areas had been circled on the lower part of the map route as points to usefully jettison a bomb load in case single planes had to return prematurely because of malfunction.

After questions and details we were directed to special briefings for the various crew positions. At the shack for radio operator we were told there should be little need for our communication capabilities. We would tend the left waist gun positions on the trip, and we would dispense the metallic chaff during the bomb run.

The chaff was a counter defense of ours. German radar sent up beams of energy which reflected back to them from our planes, as rays of light would from tiny mirrors. With measurements of time and distance, they could quickly compute our location and velocity; their projectiles were then launched with timing to explode when they met our planes. Our defense was to dispense metallic chaff from all planes to make the formation appear like a large ragged cloud to their electronic equipment instead of a precise grouping of tiny mirrors.

Dawn was beginning to show as we lugged gear to the plane. Once aboard, we started pulling on our "electric underwear" and the other clothes needed in the numbing cold of high altitude.

After takeoff, Elk and I began acquainting ourselves with a third man in the waist. He was an aerial photographer who had been in aircraft maintenance and, after "too long" a time in Italy, had decided that the only way to anticipate an eventual homecoming would be to transfer to flying status. Now on his seventeenth mission, he was counting down. He informed us we would be one of the last two planes on the bomb run. His pictures would be among the official records of our raid's success.

One other newcomer, a veteran of thirty-one trips over targets, would be our first pilot for the day. Because this was the crew's first mission, Sandy would fly copilot and Ronnie would not be with us.

Soon there were formations of our planes to our right, left, and ahead; this was the rendezvous area. They were soaring in large slow circles like hawks over a marsh and then blending into their positions in the staggered, side-by-side formation. The long line of green yarn on the briefing map had become a seemingly endless line of planes toward the north. I had never seen this many in one place at one time: obviously Rosie the riveter back home had been very busy.

I remembered that early in the war, when the odds were always against us, someone had lauded the valor of flying crews in a song with a poignant line: "One of our planes is missing." Then, as our efforts increased and many planes were expected to be lost every mission, a comedian had turned the line to mimic a supposedly surprised German radio announcer with: "Vun uff our cities iss missink!" The humor was bizarre, but the force amassed here made that implication plausible.

It was time to pull the flak jackets on. They consisted of many irregularly shaped metal plates stitched between two sheets of canvas to form a loosefitting vest. They would help prevent vital organs in the thorax from being pierced by sharp objects. Their purpose seemed primitive, identical to that of the suits of armor seen in museums from two thousand years earlier.

As we droned on toward our cruise altitude, I opened a box containing the metallic chaff to be dispensed over the target. There, just as "the woman behind the man behind the gun" and her machine had stacked them, were numerous packets of what we had called "Christmas tree tinsel" at home a few years earlier. The only difference was in the wrapper; instead of a cheery red and green, there was a plain brown band crimped to open easily in the wind.

We could afford only one packet of tinsel during all the years on my childhood farm, so we had always carefully trimmed and untrimmed the tree one strand at a time. Now, in a few hours, I would slide a packet out through a slot below my gun window every ten seconds, where the thunderous force from our propellers would blow it all over the local sky.

Elk and I continued scanning for possible German fighters. The photographer checked and rechecked his camera equipment. Time passed quickly. It was now 1220 hours; the lead planes should be over the Initial Point (IP).

Elk's big glove suddenly thumped my shoulder and then jabbed toward his window. Our formation had turned to the right after the IP. Now, many miles ahead, numerous little puffs were forming a black cloud shaped like an elongated shoebox. Our planes were flying into one end and out of the other.

I had readjusted the tinsel box and held a packet poised at the slot opening. There — the first blast! I released the chaff packet, grabbed another and started a slow count to ten. "One, two, three, four," but now the bursts were all around us. I had lost count. I slipped the packet out and snatched another.

Elk's big glove was rapidly thumping my back again. I swirled. Black debris showered toward us. The plane on our right had been hit. A flak explosion at its number three engine had blown the right wing from the body. The scene was incomprehensible — the wing tumbled over and down, and the fuselage was nosing into a dive.

Stunned, I shook the chaff packet toward Elk's mask and spun around to push it through the slot. Then another packet and another as I agonized at how those crew members couldn't survive; centrifugal force would restrain the struggles of their last long minute.

I held another packet, determined to finish a count when a blinding orange flash blew black scraps against my window. A reaction of rage misted my vision momentarily as I heard an angry bellow echo in my mask: "You're tryin' to kill us all, ya sons-a-bitches."

Counting didn't blot out the scene I was trying to eliminate, so I tried to read humor into the echo I heard with: "Of course they're trying to kill us, so we don't destroy their refineries." Another close flash, and my reaction released another packet. The bam-bam-bams and poof-poof-poofs were exploding everywhere; it was inconceivable to fly through this unscathed. After several more packets, I ripped open the reserve box of tinsel that had been intended for unexpected flak areas on the return trip.

Our plane lurched. Had we been hit? The intercom crackled. "Bombs away. Now let's get the hell out of here." That was the bombardier's voice. He compounded his error by clicking back in to say, "I wasn't supposed to add that last part."

We were already in a steep dive to our right. The dive was too steep for comfort and reminiscent of our slip-off before the crash in Arizona. But we were now flying in a sturdy bird and this was becoming the most comfortable dive I had ever experienced. I felt stupid for wondering if we had been hit.

Obviously, if you drop a ton and a half out of a plane's belly, it's going to lurch.

I took a fast glance back up at the dirty, ragged cloud we had just come out of. Residue was drifting down and away. It was ugly. But we had survived. "Thank You, God."

I glanced ahead to see our planes regrouping in the new direction. Some were missing. But our plane was joining the flight home. "Thank You, God." Now I felt sadness about those empty spots in the formation.

The intercom crackled; our pilot, Lieutenant Cord, was requesting a crew report. Good news came in from all stations. No one was hurt and no obvious damage to the aircraft could be seen. There was a unique bit of good news: Larry reported the refinery had been totally wiped out. He felt his pictures would show no need to go back to finish the job: it was finished.

I settled against the window to keep an eye out for fighters, but I had a question. Lifting my mask to one side, I shouted above engine noise to the photographer, "You've been through seventeen of these now. Was this flak typical, lighter, worse, or what?" He shook his head and forced a grin to shout back, "It wasn't light. Each mission seems to get worse, but I can't believe they could get more up there than they did."

Elk went forward to check meter readings on engine functions, etc. He asked Larry, the photographer, to cast a casual look out for fighters at his window.

I settled down again to anticipate the comfort of a safe ride home, "Thank You, God."

But nothing was comfortable. I had just been through an experience that already seemed unbelievable. I didn't want to review it, but I couldn't put it out of my mind. I had functioned poorly. I felt ashamed. I had never calmly reached a count of ten. However, the briefing officer had said that timing wasn't critical; the number was offered only as an approximate guide. My average must have been right because I had just finished the box intended for the bomb run.

I would do better next time. Could I do it again? Of course; that's why the sergeant in Arizona had slammed the "unrestricted" classification on my record. We were better able to do this now than anyone. We'd be up again next week.

Had I been brave? My legs still ached from the trembling during the bomb run. I remembered hearing bravery discussed years earlier somewhere — Boy Scouts! "Trustworthy, loyal, helpful, . . . brave, . . . and reverent." All twelve had been defined at some special award ceremony. Bravery, they said, was "*not* the absence of fear," but performance, accomplishment, or something like that "*in the presence of fear*." That was a comforting definition.

Had I been reverent? I preferred the chaplain in the song who chorused, "Praise the Lord and pass the ammunition," but I remembered Dominie

Sietsma from my childhood catechism class. He would have chided me for not seeking divine strength when that orange blast blew debris at my face. A fiendish reaction suggested that he and I fly through a flak cloud *together*: after that we would discuss what we had done wrong, or should have done instead. "Forgive me, God."

It had been nearly two hours since the target; we should be about halfway back.

The intercom crackled, "Flight engineer back there?" It was Lieutenant Cord's voice.

"No, I'm right here."

"What's wrong with our gas gauges? What's wrong with number three?"

"I don't know. I noticed that too. I'm transferring gas now."

The number three engine then sputtered and quit. Gormer popped up from the ball turret and Hartfield tumbled in from the tail. We each grabbed our chute packs and snapped the rings into the chest connectors.

"Get something to three."

"I'm trying. I'm transferring."

Number three coughed and started again.

"The bastards hit our gas lines over the target. They've just vibrated loose. They were all right. All the gauges are going down now. Navigator? Where are we?"

"We should be just east of northern Italy, over Slovenia, Yugo. We're about sixty miles north of our lines in Yugo. And sixty miles north of the Adriatic. Russia is only —." Jaris was interrupted.

"Forget Russia. Get something to two," Cord barked.

The number two engine quit.

"I'm trying. I'm transferring," Elk answered.

The four of us in the waist were nervously tying each other's GI shoe laces to the rear loops of our chute harnesses.

"Stand by to bail if necessary," Cord yelled, "We're losing altitude and control fast now. We're at sixteen thousand; a couple seconds back, we were at eighteen."

I glanced out to see our formation in the distance; we had fallen far behind and below. We would be "sitting ducks" for German fighters if any were around now. We were drifting toward our right, westerly toward Italy!

Number two started again, but then number three quit. I tried to fit my big glove through the red metal hand loop of the rip cord. I would keep the glove for warmth. If it didn't slip through out there, I could pull it off then. The face mask would slip off easily.

Number two quit again. Then number four — and one — and there was a long moment of unbelievable quiet without engines, only the sound of the wind that buffeted us about in our glide.

And then the terrible clanging of the bail-out bell crashed the quiet and jangled on and on and on.

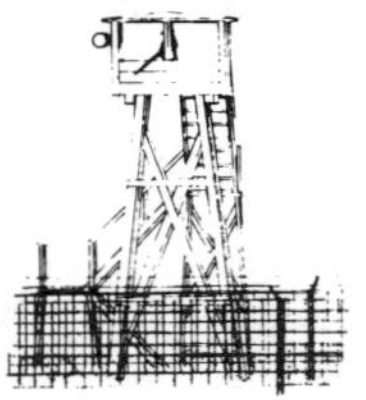

Chapter 6

Don't Take Me to Your Leader

Chilling winds hissed angrily when Hartfield tripped the latch and swung the camera hatch door up from the floor of the plane. He and the others stepped aside leaving the opening directly in front of me with bottomless clouds rolling a thousand feet below. This was no time to hesitate.

I remembered the recommended procedure from the instruction session: "Crouch at edge of hatch, bend head down between knees, wrap arms around head to protect it from possible bumps on edges and somersault forward through opening." While starting into the position, I also remembered I wouldn't be able to do that — I had never successfully turned somersaults on the living room floor as a child, nor happily tumbled the two feet from a diving board into water.

I sat at the edge and dropped my feet through the hole instead. The wind straightened my legs toward the tail section, I forced my head down, grabbed the hatch edges and threw myself out. There was a cold turbulence as I started the count, "One, two," but that seemed senseless; my chute could not tangle with the plane which was already many yards away; a more important concern was whether the chute would open.

My body was falling toward the left when I rammed the glove into the metal hand loop. They had said, "Don't 'pull' your ripcord, *jerk* it; then the release pins will slide out even if they are corroded or slightly bent." I yanked with all the strength in my arm. The little square pilot-chute snapped open, billows of whiteness rolled out and flashed upward, there was a loud "plop" above me and I was bouncing in the chute harness like an infant in a jump seat.

I had been intensely watching a red line which was tracing upward. It started near my chest, was momentarily overshadowed by the opening of the chute and continued much higher. Curiously, it formed an arch and was coming back down. Suddenly, several yards beyond my reach when it returned, I identified the big red hand loop of my ripcord.

It had slipped from grip during the mighty yank. I was saddened. That was the part they would have let me keep. "That's my ripcord," could have been the answer many years later when someone asked what that item was on the wall of the den; now I wouldn't even have proof of the jump. The ripcord would instead merely corrode away for decades in the woods on the foothills of the Eastern Alps. I had bungled a once-in-a-lifetime opportunity.

When it vanished in the clouds below, I realized I would be dropping at that awesome speed if the handle hadn't been yanked adequately. I looked up to see a gorgeous gigantic white umbrella, as if an angel had formed its wings into a huge protective circle. Then I remembered there were other crew members.

A second body was dropping from the hatch of the plane now a quarter-mile away. Its chute opened and snapped it erect. Only a few seconds had passed since my jump. There should have been little time to think, but, retrospectively, that event-filled sequence seemed long and unforgettable.

My watch showed 1430 hours. Five minutes previously we had still been anticipating an uneventful ride home.

Now a body tumbled from the bomb bay — they had opened those doors! Another dropped from the camera hatch. One somersaulted from the bay — he had done it right! Another fell from the hatch and two more from the bay.

The plane was gliding down and toward its right; now it leveled slightly as it disappeared into cloud cover. Obviously, Cord was still fighting the flight controls. Two others were still in the plane with him.

Eight bodies dangled from shroud lines along a gentle curve extending over a mile. One waved an arm. Then we all waved to each other, stopped waving and affirmed the greetings again with another exchange. We then settled into the clouds.

The new world was white and windy. Large snowflakes blew horizontally and swirled in all directions. Visibility seemed to be only a few feet, but I could see my chute twenty feet above. Strong gusts repeatedly collapsed the chute to two-thirds of its normal diameter. Suddenly, everything cleared. The other seven reappeared and we jubilantly exchanged waves again. Another white cloud blanket several thousand feet down covered whatever might be below.

A different thought terrified me suddenly. Our navigator had said we should be over Slovenia, Yugo, but we had been near the Italian border and were drifting westward. I remembered Leebe's fate. Could there be White Guards waiting down there?

More urgent things needed to be reviewed first. The cloud blanket below could be a dense ground fog. This "emergency chute" would not provide the soft landing of the larger ones used by the Troopers. Instructors had said the landing would be like a jump from a second story window: "Bend the knees slightly, absorb half the shock with your feet, your knees will buckle and you'll take the balance on your rear end as you roll backward."

I settled through several thin layers of whiteness which provided an idea of my rapid rate of descent. And then the world turned calm white.

Dark spots were appearing! The ground was only several hundred feet below. Thoughts raced at top speed again. There was a village of stone buildings a mile to the left. A meadow bordered the village, and I was floating toward a sparsely wooded valley beyond. Large tree limbs raced upward past me.

My eyes opened. I was lying on my back — I had done it right. There had been tremendous jolt and a short burst of bright amber stars, but it seemed only a second before I was recollecting my senses.

I took a moment to scan the sky and appreciate being the most fortunate person on earth. My watch showed 1440 hours. The three-mile ride had taken ten minutes.

As I sat up, a small creek a few yards away brought all of the survival instructions to mind. I must first get out of the area in case my descent had been seen; with the low cloud cover, odds of not having been noticed were in my favor.

I would hide the chute, put my shoes on and walk in the creek in case they put hounds out to track me; downstream would be away from the village. Then I could hide out overnight. It would be safer to make a contact with someone in a rural area; preferably one person alone. If this were Italy, I must head toward Yugo. In Yugo, I must avoid Chetniks and get with Partisans.

The chute was draped across low brush behind me. I would gather it into a bundle. But an excruciating pain shot through my right arm as I rose to my feet. The arm wouldn't move. An attempt to lift it with my other hand caused similar pain. How could my arm have been broken?

The answer appeared in deep scuff marks on a small tree stump beside the spot where my back had hit the ground. Bark and slivers from the stump were imbedded in the sleeve of my jacket. After a moment of regret, I was glad that my head had not hit the stump instead.

I had just begun gathering up chute material when I heard excited human gabbling. A dozen men appeared over the crest of a slope fifty yards up the valley. They stopped, pointed, yelled among themselves and dashed toward me followed by a horde of others. In seconds, two hundred of them surrounded me. Most wore parts of military garb and many carried guns.

Their babble subsided when a man directly in front of me appeared to be asking a question. I remembered to force a smile as I shook my head negatively. Another tried a different question. Then, from a few rows back, one asked, "Cop-ee-toe Eye-tal-yon?"

I understood that and it worried me, but I smiled as I replied, "No capeesh Eye-tal-yon."

Before I could say more, their questions popped in from all directions.

"Spraken Doytch?"

"No. Nyen Doytch."

"Spon-yole?"

"No. No Spon-yole."

"Fron-say?"

"No. No Fron-say."

Not wanting to continue sounding negative, I interrupted with a firm but friendly, "English, English."

After a shocked silence, a man uttered a quiet and seemingly disheartened, "Een-glee-ski?"

Others responded similarly.

Feeling that the language was being confused with nationality, I added, "American, American."

The attitude improved.

"Amerikon!" one confirmed.

"Merryconski?" another questioned with some surprise.

"Melicano," somebody chuckled.

"Amerikonisher," another emphasized.

With a variety of dialects, or at least responses, they seemed to be agreeing that they now knew my nationality.

Our location was still my foremost concern. Directing my attention to the man who had asked if I understood Italian, I gestured toward the ground and said, "Is this Italy?" He laughed and shook his head negatively. I felt he might be laughing at my jabber and indicating he didn't understand. That was confirmed when I received the same response after asking, "Is this Yugoslavia?"

I reached down to get the survival map pack from one of my shin pockets. Because I could use only one hand, I held the plastic box between my feet to open it and found I had picked the wrong pack. Onlookers uttered various noises expressing awe and amazement as they observed gauze bandages, adhesive tape, water-purification tablets, and so on.

When I straightened up because my arm hurt, something that felt like the muzzle of a gun pressed against my back. A cautious turn revealed a teen-age boy with a rifle slung in the crook of his arm. He moved it and appeared to apologize with gestures indicating he had become careless because of interest in the survival pack.

There were further expressions of wonder as I unfolded a colorful cloth map from the other shin pack. But I could get no one interested in the meanings of inscriptions on the map which could confirm our location; they were overwhelmed instead by the map's material and brilliance.

By now, I surmised that these were peasants from the village who thought I was showing them my accouterments. Their military jackets, caps, and trousers were merely remnants from former military uniforms worn for warmth in combination with other crudely knit materials. Because all were similarly dressed, I hadn't noticed initially that there were many women in the crowd.

Suddenly, a man took my left arm and pointed up the hill toward the way from which they had come. I groaned and pulled away as another took my right arm. When I showed him the scuff marks on my jacket and the stump, he understood and explained to others how the arm had been hurt. Several of them collected the parachute and picked up the boxes and the map. All seemed anxious to proceed to the village.

I felt very wary of the group's intentions for me, but I realized despondently how difficult it would be to escape from this involvement at this time. None among them wore signs saying which ones were Partisans, which might be Chetniks, or which of them could be White Guards.

The village appeared on the next horizon as the man who had linked his arm into mine led us out of the valley. Not a word of the gabble from the crowd behind us was understandable, but I drew hope from a realization that it didn't sound like anything I had heard in Italy.

I tried to recall my brief aerial view of the local geography. It would be dark in two hours and anything I remembered could be helpful if an escape attempt became possible. I knew there was a large open space at the center of the village with an irregular arrangement of crooked streets leading to it like spokes in a wheel.

The dirt path we were on suddenly changed to a narrow cobblestone street between two-story buildings made from large gray stones and white mortar. In two blocks, we stopped at the edge of the open area I had seen from the descent. It was a circular city block of cobblestones enclosed by houses like those along the street. There seemed to be no one else in the village.

The people who had been behind us crowded forward for a better view. A messenger they appointed walked briskly across the opening and disappeared through a heavy wooden door on the far side. Those remaining around me whispered excitedly to each other. My thoughts annoyed me by repeating, "This is where they will execute you for illegal entry into their weird world."

The heavy door reopened and the messenger trotted back to take his place in line with the peasants. Then an older man draped in a long black robe came out and ambled slowly toward us. He had a cleric's collar. I felt it might be best to be whatever religion he was. When directly in front of me, he paused and made hand motions which could have been a sign of the cross, or a blessing — or a last rite.

Then he slowly said, "Do you speak English?

"Yes, Sir," I answered."

Still spellbound from his ceremonious activities as I waited for the response, I suddenly realized he had articulated my language perfectly.

I asked excitedly, "May I ask a question, Sir?"

He nodded and smiled approvingly.

"Is this Yugoslavia?"

My spirit sank when he slowly shook his head negatively.

"Then this is Italy?" I questioned despondently.

After another slow negative, I said, "It must be one or the other because we're certainly south of the Austrian border." As the same response continued, I returned his question, "Do you speak English?" He didn't. His four-word repertoire was perfect, but useless to me.

He made more ceremonious hand gestures and turned to amble slowly back to his door. We waited, reverently I presumed, until he had reentered. From the happy little mutterings in the crowd, I deduced that everyone was delighted that he and I had exchanged words. I felt their approval was a good sign.

Some of the crowd dispersed as our leader took us along the edge of the circle and down another street. We turned into a courtyard and jostled through the side door of a building, along a hallway and up two flights of stairs to enter a large room. A fully uniformed man sat at an old wooden desk next to a window in the far corner. Shabby couches occupied the two alternate corners and a potbellied stove stood along a wall across the room from another window.

A roaring fire in the stove had the room uncomfortably warm compared to the chilly December weather outside. I was still heavily dressed for the subzero temperatures at 25,500 feet, I hadn't had anything to eat or drink since breakfast twelve hours earlier, and my arm tortured me constantly. As many people forced their way around me, they inhaled the room's oxygen, the temperature increased, and I slumped fainting to the floor.

I responded to damp cloths being patted to my face by two ladies leaning over me. My jackets and shirt had been opened and a cool breeze blew in through a window.

A man on his knees beside me smiled and said, "How are you now?

I was still too weak to care, but I managed, "I'm fine."

"My name is John," he said, "I went through New York and I worked ten years in Detroit. Where are you from there?"

"West. Across Lake Michigan."

"Chicago?" he beamed, apparently proud of his geography.

"No. In the state above Chicago. Over a hundred miles north."

"I don't know that state."

The ladies' cold cloths had restored my survival instincts and I interrupted his next question with, "Is this Yugoslavia?"

"Yes, you are in Yugoslavia."

"Tell this guy to leave my arm alone." I begged, "It's broken and it hurts terribly."

"He is the doctor," John said, "They got him because they knew your arm was broken and they got me because I could talk your English to you."

"These people seem friendly," I suggested cautiously.

"Yes, they are all very friendly to you," John assured, "You have no need to fear. They are delighted to be able to help you."

The doctor's large fingers, now inside my jacket, continued probing the sore shoulder as he suddenly babbled to John.

"The doctor says your arm is not broken. The shoulder is dislocated. He wants you to get on the couch so he can fix it," John informed, "I must get back now. I am working. But I will see you again in less than three hours," he continued. "Right after six I am through working. I will come directly here. These people have many questions they wish me to ask you, and you and I have much to talk about."

My new friend, a crooked little man with a crooked little smile, continued waving kindly as he backed hurriedly through the crowd and out the door.

I had ample help while sliding out of the jackets, the electric underwear, the flight boots, and the wool shirt. Though sixty years old, the doctor, with the size and physique of a football player, acted more like a general as he directed preparations to fix the shoulder. While I lay on the couch, he positioned six of his helpers' hands on my chest and two more on each hip. He then wrapped his massive hands around my right wrist and braced one of his large booted feet against the edge of the couch.

Following a final command, the assistants smiled broadly through unkempt beards and brown and broken teeth as they pressed my body firmly against the couch. I bellowed like a calf being branded as the doctor slowly twisted the arm and pulled it into place. Those few seconds had seemed like forever. He nodded approval after additional probing and then talked to a young lady who would be my nurse for the next couple of hours.

Fortunately, I didn't know then that the arm's disability would distress me for several months and that it would take twenty-five years to learn to protect it from the night's cold to avoid morning stiffness.

The doctor and several others left.

My new nurse returned to me with scissors and neatly cut open the sleeve of my underwear from the wrist to the seam above the shoulder. Now I understood why the doctor had drawn his finger up that line on my arm while he talked to her, but I was sorry because I felt I would need the sleeve when I faced the December weather again later.

The young lady was very shy as she first placed a hot rag on my shoulder from water she brought from the stove. She seemed embarrassed while apparently trying to ask if it was too hot. She appreciated my approval.

She was skinny, had a sallow complexion and stringy brown hair. I remembered American civilians complaining about the inconveniences of meat and sugar rationing, and the girls saying they certainly couldn't look their best with war shortages of silks and nylons. But this girl hadn't had adequate nourishment, probably had very little access to soap, and certainly had no cosmetics.

She gained confidence from my appreciation while replacing the cloths with warmer ones. Later, she enjoyed our exchange of questions and answers in our own languages while neither knew what the other had said. She was most pleased when I liked her soft singing of what was probably a Yugoslavian lullaby or folk song. Despite the absence of grooming aids, she became beautiful very soon.

There were always a dozen or more persons in the room as new visitors came and others left. All were curious and amazed at my parachute, clothes, and equipment on the other couch. Their nods and greetings toward me were invariably friendly. Two of them, each at different times, approached me with laughs and gestures indicating they had something funny to share, and then asked, "You Chicago gangster?" I was surprised that America's social misbehaviors of the '30s had taken precedence in the world's opinion of us.

Suddenly, amid a small group of escorts, Hartfield limped in. He had sprained an ankle by taking too much of his weight on one foot as he landed. The remaining six were brought in, each by other escorts, within the next half-hour. No one else had been injured. All had had generally similar experiences around the area. That explained why the town had been left unattended; its inhabitants had all raced out in different directions to find the men they had seen coming down with parachutes.

Because of their absence, we deduced that those who had been in the plane as it disappeared into the clouds were Cord, the pilot for this mission; Sandy, acting copilot; and Jaris, the navigator.

Our group's prime concern now was how to get out of German-occupied territory and eventually back to Italy. The other crew members surmised we were temporarily safe, but had heard no meaningful English. I related what John had said and that he would be back in another hour; with the impending darkness in our favor, it seemed best to wait for his advice.

One of our curious visitors was particularly interested in my life preserver on the couch. It was the flat flexible type that hung loosely around the neck. This type was always fondly called a Mae West by servicemen because, when its pin was pulled, compressed gas from a small cartridge inflated two large air bags on the wearer's chest. When the visitor eventually pulled the pin, he and the fifteen watching him fled to the door as the gas hissed quickly into the air bags. They returned cautiously, even more amazed at the Americans' gadgetry.

As a softer level of hissing continued, we Americans became curious. A malfunction, one of the very few ever found in our equipment, allowed a leak to deflate the air bags. I shuddered, remembering how anxiously we had hoped that our engines might keep running; if they had continued for another twenty minutes, we would have been over the Adriatic Sea — and I would have been the one who pulled that pin.

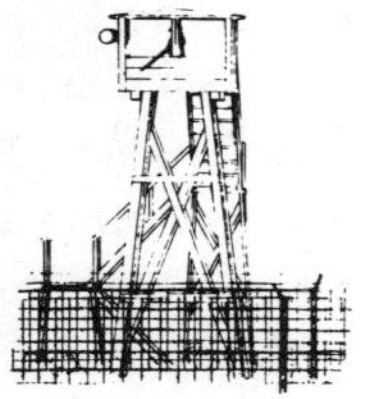

Chapter 7

The Ljubljana Jail

We had begun to feel secure in the care and comfort of our snug upper chamber. Darkness was covering the land outside. Our room was electrically lighted and, probably because there was nothing of military significance in the surrounding kilometers, there were no blackout shutters on the windows. John would return soon with further advice.

Strangely, a change in mood among the locals in the room was becoming increasingly obvious. They continued exchanging short questions, but there were only shrugs for answers. They seemed concerned and, more likely, frightened. There had been occasional telephone calls during the afternoon which the uniformed man at the desk had answered promptly; we felt the change in attitude had followed a phone message.

My nurse hurriedly peeled a long thread from a spool and slipped it into a needle. With a finger inside the sleeve and others sliding along the edges she had cut earlier, her hands formed a seam at the rate and rhythm of a machine. I stared entranced as the stitches fell into perfect intervals. After neatly trimming a final knot, she dashed to the window, shook a bony fist toward the outside darkness, and returned to verbalize apparent anger while wiping tears.

The members of our crew all agreed we would grab our jackets and disappear outside at any sign of real danger. On our decision to leave everything, I borrowed the nurse's scissors to take a souvenir. Although the left-handed effort was clumsy, I managed to cut a one-foot-square piece from my parachute.

Pocket knives had snapped open and waited in polite hands all about the room until I nodded to indicate I had finished. Within the next minute, the balance of the chute was divided among the local Yugoslavians, who participated in a cutting and tearing melee. There had been no fights or wounds and almost everyone came away with a piece that seemed to please him; some were large enough to make into clothing. No one argued about unequal share sizes.

Suddenly the door opened and two men in green uniforms stepped in, tensely gripping poised rifles. Pistols hung in holsters at their sides as they nervously glanced about the crowd. A quiet shock fell across the room. They relaxed and slid the rifle-slings to their shoulders as it became obvious that there were no guns confronting them.

The leader stepped toward our crew and questioned, "Boom? Boom Doytch-londt? Boom Shermany?"

We stared at him in mute disbelief.

He forced a laugh and continued, "Ya. Ya. Goot. Goot. Undt now you vill come mit unce."

We continued to stare.

He appeared amused, forced another chuckle and added, "Ya. Vee take you."

Several of us shock our heads negatively.

He patted his rifle authoritively, chuckled again and confirmed, "Ya, vee come to take you mit unce."

His partner rapped a hand sharply against his rifle, leered and nodded agreement.

One of our crew muttered, "I don't understand."

After a condescending grin and more tapping to show his rifle's authority, the spokesman jabbed a finger emphatically toward each of us and said, "For you der vor iss oafer."

We understood his words, but were unable to accept the message. Our lower gunner lifted his leather helmet and flung it angrily against the floor while growling, "I didn't think the son of a bitch was gonna end this way." While another of the crew quietly suggested, "At ease," the would-be captors stepped back, unslung their rifles, and glared. We had learned our first lesson in dealing with the enemy: the minor outburst had increased their hostility.

The leader gestured toward our feet and ordered, "You shtay. Vee talk," as he then pointed across the room.

While they talked to the man at the desk, we communicated among ourselves in whispers whenever they weren't watching. Though the desk attendant wore a different uniform, they spoke fluently to each other in some other language.

Our concern was escape. Collective memories told us the only exit from the building was the way we had entered. We agreed that an attempt to dash through the doorway would be fatal; some of us would certainly be shot in such an effort.

With limited time, one crew member hurriedly summarized our discussion:

"Check this. When they come back, we casually pretend that we're accepting whatever they suggest. We turn to our right just outside this door, left down the hall to the first flight of stairs, follow the landing to the second flight, and turn right in the long hall downstairs. There, each one counts how many are ahead of him as we approach the outside door. The last man out yells 'Go' at the top of his lungs when his last foot hits the ground outside. We split like lightning, eight ways into the dark, and these dim-wits won't have a thing to shoot at."

We had all listened intently and we all agreed.

"Got it."

"Right."

"Check."

We were now free to begin pretending to act casual.

The nurse came to our group offering hard brown crackers and sardines with an offensive odor. We declined politely, but only because our emotions were preoccupied with the intense excitement of our escape plans.

"Now vee go," the leader ordered as he returned from the other end of the room. "Two by two," he kept repeating as he made his point by pushing us into two columns facing the door. I was shoved into the first position in the line on the left. I felt the insistence on a military exit put me in an advantageous position. The two guards followed our columns.

My pulse pounded wildly as I reviewed personal plans while we proceeded into the hallway. At the yell of "Go" I would dash to the left and retrace my path to the valley. It was the only way out of the village that I was familiar with, and I felt I could find it in the dark. Then I would walk in the creek. Before tracking dogs were put out in the morning, I could be miles away from the area.

As we stepped from the landing to the lower flight of stairs, I noticed a row of black boots against the opposite wall. A voice below gargled, "Achtoong," and the boots closed into pairs. Fifteen guards from the stairs to the end of the hall had drawn their rifle muzzles toward the wall at that command. Now their squad leader grunted another command releasing them from their rigid stance so they could jest and snicker as we walked in front of them.

A steep ramp led from the door's threshold to the platform of a large truck that had been backed to the door. Five additional guards stood along each side of the ramp. After we had climbed the ramp, five more on the truck met us with abusive attitudes and harsh remarks as they shoved us to our knees and hips on the floor.

The truck's tailgate, which had served as the ramp, was repositioned at the rear of the platform and all guards climbed aboard. We huddled near the center among the sixty boots of our captors who crowded along the railings. All were armed and some carried large flashlights used briefly to confirm a final count.

The driver proceeded without headlights; Europeans had learned to function well in the dark. The truck was old and particularly noisy while crossing the cobblestones. Our captors were in a boisterous mood. They seemed to be congratulating each other on the success of their current conquest, or perhaps they were just practicing their role as part of the "master race."

We joggled from the cobblestones to a curved country lane and finally to what felt like a smooth, surfaced road. After a few miles, Foggerty relayed a whispered question from the other crew members: "Have you got your Forty-five with you?"

I whispered back, "Yes. I put it in my jacket pocket before we jumped, but there's only the seven rounds of ammo in the magazine," and I waited for the whisper relay to complete its circuit.

"There's only one other one, but there's no other ammo. Everybody thinks these guys would kill us if they found guns on us now."

"I agree."

"Can you get rid of yours?"

"I think so. I'll try."

I carefully maneuvered my arm between the boots, slid the pistol under the side railing and gave it a gentle nudge. There was too much truck noise to hear it hit the road, but I had seen it drop over the edge.

Then another whisper came back: "The other one's gone. They pushed it over the edge of the platform."

"Mine's gone too. I did the same thing," I answered.

"Good."

As we rumbled on into the night, I despondently remembered how elated I had been eight months earlier in South Dakota when I was awarded the classification of "Expert" in the use of the weapon I had just nudged overboard.

Silhouettes of large buildings became discernible against the night sky after a long ride through country hills. We were entering a blacked-out city. Barely visible light could be seen in the lower halves of hooded headlights on occasional vehicles.

Our guards ushered us into the lobby of one of the more modern buildings; two of them led the way around a stairwell to the sixth floor while several others followed.

In the middle of a long hallway, we were directed to wait against a wall while our leader stepped up to a door just ahead. The door opened after his knock, he took a brief step backward, snapped his arm into the Nazi salute and said, "Heil Hitler." The salute was returned by someone in the doorway and the guard muttered a terse report about "ocht mon."

I was not emotionally prepared to witness the obvious sincerity of that exchange. We had seen such antics only in films and mimicked them in sarcastic humor in high school less than two years earlier.

After being beckoned forward, we were shuffled into a line just inside the doorway of a large room, and I was less prepared for the scene we encountered as we entered. A brilliant red flag with a jet black swastika in a dazzling white center circle covered one end of the room from the high ceiling down to a series of folds that embraced a five-foot-high bust portrait of Hitler. Paintings of two other selected Nazi party leaders hung in smaller frames from a lower level at the sides.

There were twenty elegant wooden desks spaciously arranged in five rows on a highly polished hardwood floor. Only three of the desk chairs were occupied, probably because it was after eight o'clock on a Saturday evening. The men were dressed in black uniforms.

Without looking up from his work, one of them excused the remaining guards. This left our crew silently overlooking the office area from behind a low ornamental fence.

My mind kept pretending we were bit-players in a scene being filmed for an American "propaganda movie." I remembered having been one of the high school "critics" who would have concluded that this setting was "probably overdone by Hollywood."

Finally, one of the three Germans pushed his chair back and stood at his desk. He appeared to be in his fifties. Except for his stature of only five feet and the monocle in front of his right eye, he oddly resembled Hitler. He seemed to be timing the clicks from his heel plates as he paced slowly through a gate in the little fence. He leered silently up to our faces during his parade past us and back. He suddenly stopped and demanded something that sounded like, "Who shcrrrched you?"

Bewildered while attempting to be helpful, someone quietly said, "He asked, 'Who scratched you?' but I don't know what he means."

Our discussion seemed to annoy him. When he repeated his demand, someone else said, "No, he's saying, 'Who scorched you?' whatever that means."

"No, he's trying to ask about who searched us!"

"Nobody. Nobody."

"Vot? You have not been shcrrrched?" he bellowed as if we had betrayed some trusted procedure.

His monocle flew from his eye to the end of its cord as he swung around to shout an order. The other two Germans scurried out through doors in the left end of the room muttering, "Ya vool, Herr Hauptmann, ya vool." The Herr glowered at us again for several seconds and then briskly followed the others, leaving us unguarded in the spacious room.

Our bombardier broke the silence with a shocked whisper, "I've still got a copy of the flight plan in my shirt pocket." As he unfolded the sheet, someone said, "Tear it up; we'll eat it." After three quick rips into halves, quarters and eighths, we each grabbed a piece, duplicated the motions and popped the scraps into our mouths just before the officers returned with two shabbily uniformed goons. They hurriedly frisked us and nodded to indicate we were unarmed.

The goons left the room, the other Germans returned to their desks, and we stood silently for what seemed to be an interminable twenty minutes.

One of the goons finally returned, talked briefly with the monocled Hauptmann, and led Berry, our flight officer, into the room to our left; after another twenty minutes, Berry was walked behind our line-up to a room on our right. The staff sergeant was taken second. He had earned his rank in an extended service period prior to transfer to our training group. The rest of us were still corporals. I was relieved to be chosen sixth after the two-hour stand.

Only a single desk stood at the center of the large adjoining room. An officer sat behind a typewriter at a recessed end of the desk; although the room was unheated, his military jacket hung over a chair. A sentinel with a bayoneted rifle stood near his desk.

The goon hurried me to a small table near a side wall where his partner waited. He drummed his finger tips on a table there and said, "Poot all in pockets here undt zen undress all clothes to naked." His co-worker nodded, "Ya. Vee look you like shpies."

They fingered over and into all body parts, purportedly checking for concealed evidence which might reveal spy activity. Because of the physical indecencies, I was too preoccupied with embarrassment to analyze motives at the time; however, I have felt since that the humiliation was the actual purpose, as a preconditioning for interrogation by the officer.

After flexing all seams in what was called a "check for photo films," I was handed my undershorts and told, "Put dis on to respect officer, undt zen report to desk."

In the next few seconds I tried to recall what we had been told regarding behavior in case of capture by the enemy; the part about no information beyond name, rank, and serial number was easy, but the other things hadn't seemed important before.

There had been something about trying to retain personal dignity while respecting their humanity; I thought I remembered a salute was appropriate when formally addressing a military officer. There had been nothing about how to appear dignified while walking across an icy floor with bare feet, or how to prevent body shivers from being obvious when wearing only a loincloth.

I was instantly chagrined to receive the Nazi salute with a "Heil Hitler" in return for my gesture of military respect.

"Name?" the interrogator snapped.

I pronounced and spelled it as his typewriter rattled it onto the paper.

"Rank?
"Corporal."
"Serial number?"
"Three, six, eight, two, six, seven, zero."
"Age?"
"I'm sorry, Sir, but my country's orders require that I give no information beyond my name, rank and service serial number."

He leaned back in his chair, forced a condescending grin and said, "We take you in order of rank for obvious reasons. Your officer saw the need for the few questions we have and answered them all very cooperatively. Likewise, your noncommissioned officer and subsequently, all the others." His English was perfect with a crisp pronunciation that we Americans called a British accent. He leaned forward again, poised his fingers over the keys and emphatically said, "Now let us get on with this! Age?"

"I'm sorry, Sir. I'm allowed to give only —"

He interrupted with, "How could your age possibly be of any military significance? You are a soldier; I am a soldier. We can at least respect each other's roles in our military duties. I am here working very late at night just to try to help identify you people so we can treat you fairly," He cocked his fingers over the keys again and firmly shouted, "Age?"

"I'm sorry, Sir. I —"

"You idiots," he bellowed as he slapped a flat hand on the desk top. "We are trying to save the world from Bolshevism, and you are doing everything conceivable to impede our efforts!" His startling whack to the desk had involuntarily contracted muscles that jolted my heels an inch off the floor in a very undignified jerk. I now understood why the Nazi worked without a jacket in an unheated room — his antics kept him warm.

"We need this information," he shouted, "to prove you are military people; otherwise you are spies. We are the Gestapo, and you know what we do with spies."

"No Sir, I don't know what you —"

"Vot?" he shrieked, "You claim to be a soldier and you have not heard of the Geshtapo!" This was his first slur from otherwise perfect English pronunciation. Until then, I had assumed he was an adept actor; but that reaction seemed involuntary.

"Of course, I've heard of the Gestapo, Sir. I meant to say, 'I don't know what you do —' "

"We cut off your heads," he gasped as his extended index finger slashed across his throat. "Age?"

"I'm sorry, Sir. I cannot —"

"I will enter your age as twenty," he snarled with a quick glance upward.

I nodded to confirm that I understood his intention. When his typewriter tapped twice, I wondered if I could be considered a traitor merely because he had guessed right.

"What was your crew function on your bomber?"

"I'm sorry, Sir, but, as I've said, I'm only allowed to give —"

"You've already given more than your stated restrictions," he retorted with a sarcastic grin.

"No, sir. My nod was not intended to confirm your estimate, but only —"

"You were on a bomber, weren't you?"

"I'm sorry, Sir, but I must insist —"

"The reliable people who brought you in said you have parachuted from a bomber. Would you rather be considered a spy?"

"No Sir, but I cannot —"

"Go," he growled, pointing to the little table where his goons waited with my clothes, "I can't waste the entire night on one obstinate captive who appears to care nothing about the system or himself. I cannot be responsible for what will happen to you."

I felt too exhausted to dress, but the only relief from the indecent heckling of the goons was to get on to whatever was next. As I hurried along behind the remaining crew members, I realized why the previous ones had appeared so pale and weary. In the next room, I rejoined the first five. We waited in chairs around a long conference table under the glaring surveillance of new guards.

After the last crew member rejoined us, we were hustled to the building's basement for another long wait until our interrogator suddenly entered the room carrying a submachine gun.

He said we would be taking "a little walk of several blocks to the local jail here in Ljubljana." He then grinned diabolically while making "a few points" about the piece he was carrying: "This is the item that you Americans have so appropriately dubbed the 'grease gun.' By comparison, your Thompson submachine gun seems like a poor substitute for this weapon."

He had always enjoyed firing the grease gun, he said, partly because of the intriguing notion that the minds of men were now able to design these instruments with capabilities that the minds themselves could not fully comprehend: even after short bursts at range practice, he always counted many more spent casings than he could believe had been fired.

He explained that we would walk in a very close group, essentially touching each other, that he would call out directions from the rear, and that our eyes would adjust quickly to the dark.

For the one of us who had asked if we didn't have rights under rules of the Geneva Convention, the answer was "yes," said sarcastically, but we shouldn't concern ourselves over his compliance with those rules; if anyone deviated from the close grouping, he would enjoy some night practice with the grease gun, and his entry in the records would merely say the prisoners had attempted escape.

Several other guards closed in behind us as we walked out into the dark city.

Most of the time, we just sat quietly, bewildered, on our bunks in the third-floor cell of the Ljubljana jail. We were desperately hungry. Although survival preoccupied us, our thoughts were always frustrated by the realization that we could make no plans. If there were to be a future, someone else would control it. So we drew short conclusions from events in our immediate past instead.

Typical conversations with long intervals between retorts or comments were as follows:

"Never trust people who are trying to be nice to you; they're stupid."

"Most of those people were Partisans, but that son of a bitch at the desk was a Chetnik."

"You don't know that."

"You don't know that he wasn't either.

"He was just collecting his payoff."

"You don't know that either."

"None of us know anything. If we did, we wouldn't be in this hole."

"Do you guys have to keep arguing?"

Our staff sergeant surprised us on the third morning with a very different sort of conversation as he smiled and optimistically announced, "Fellows, I've made a decision. I might get all shot to ribbons trying, but I've decided to get the hell out of this place. The next time that door opens, I'm going through it so goddam fast everybody in the way won't know what happened. When I get outside, I'll just keep runnin', or dodgin' bullets or whatever it takes, but at least I'll get a chance to run."

The rest of us all protested at once; we then slowed to understandable advice. We insisted he couldn't possibly live through the long run down the first hall, certainly not the next, or the stairs, and there would be no unlocked doors out. We reminded him that we heard the guards in the hall constantly and that our door opened only during daylight hours, at noon, when they came in to empty our slop bucket and measure out our cup of cabbage water.

We respected the twenty-eight-year-old veteran and his five years of service experience, but we weren't sure he was listening. Mostly, he just chewed his cheek and stared at the wall. After a long silence an hour later, when we had exhausted ways to express our feelings, he quietly said, "I suppose."

On the fourth morning, our interrogator came in to assure us that he was a Nazi and that they were winning the war, and to explain that they could have accomplished great things for the world if we hadn't entered the war in opposition to their efforts.

The fifth morning brought five new guards, whose leader stepped in to say, "Vee take you."

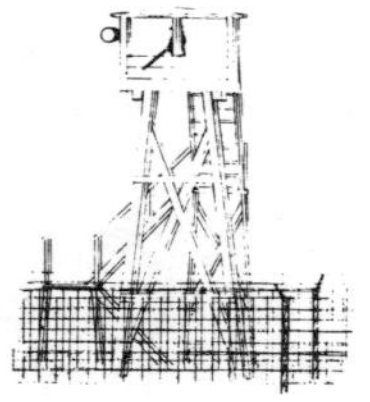

Chapter 8

Wartime Tourism

The walk to the Ljubljana train station was a welcome relief from the dirty gray walls and the stench from our slop bucket.

A mixed crowd of civilian and German military personnel waited outside the depot for transportation. They recognized us as American prisoners when our guards marched us onto an elevated loading platform; they jeered and laughed, and the younger ones tossed stones. The stones were not intended to hurt physically; they were the size of walnuts and bounced harmlessly among our feet, but they made a point.

Our travels started in civilian accommodations. The eight of us occupied two booths in a rail passenger coach with our guards across the aisle. As the train hugged the mountainsides, tiny villages two thousand feet down in the valley provided scenes that were breathtaking. If ten guns hadn't been watching us, we would have considered the views beautiful.

We arrived in a city named Wien late in the evening. They pronounced it "Veen," the city our geography books had called "Vienna." We were in Austria, the country of Hitler's birth, and we soon discovered that hatred toward us was far more intense here than two hundred miles south in Yugoslavia.

Following a long walk to a different station, we found that the railway out of the city was "Allas kaput," meaning damaged beyond use after American bombings. We were to wait outside near a dim streetlight where a convoy of trucks was convening to take the gathering crowd to a place beyond the damage.

A uniformed officer who joined the crowd looked quizzically toward us and then approached our lead guard. After several harsh words, he became intense, then violent, and then physically uncontrollable. He jumped high off the ground and his fists flailed above his head as he called us "ghott fer dompta shvine-hoondt Amerikonisher terror fliegers" and continued swearing other hostilities. Our guards closed together in front of us.

We already understood enough German to know he had called us "goddam pig-dog American terror fliers." A glance at the crowd revealed that everyone agreed and would be glad to help him tear us into shreds.

Our leader pulled the guards together in front of the maniac, stepped back toward us, and said, "Follow me." The nine of us faked a casual walk behind the first truck, then sprinted across the street, hurdled several hedges, and slid to our knees in the snow behind evergreen foundation plantings at a church a block away.

After some moments to catch our breath, our guard lectured, "Now you see vot feelings you make here. You are lucky to have us as guards. Our job iss best vork in our country today. I intend to deliver you to interrogation center; if I do not, my intent may look suspicious. I am older man. I do not vont to be sent to front to fight. But, if you vont to live, you must cooperate."

He gasped for air and continued, "Our people hear rumors that vee treat you better than other prisoners. The rumors are true, but vee cannot tell them that. Every day now vee are hit harder by you than anybody ever before. Ven vee get down from truck or train, I vill shout commands at you and you must obey. Hurry into two lines. Never look up. Look at ground. Look tired. Some vill try to talk to you; never talk. I vill explain you to them; I vill say you can't talk because vee work you to death. Vee must go now."

We trotted a circuitous route back to what had become a twenty-truck convoy. Our leader said, "No, not in last truck; they would look for you here." The third truck from the end had a canvas cover; he said, "In here, on knees in front. Don't talk. In dark, they vill think you are dumb. I vill vait out here for other guards. They vill look here."

Soon there were excited voices from the crowd bustling along beside the convoy to claim riding space. When those who were boarding our truck bumped into us, we trembled in the dark as they tried to converse. But the problem of packing too many passengers into inadequate space soon became a larger concern than our lack of response.

While many were left without transportation, we hustled out of the city with determined passengers clinging to running boards.

Fortunately, I didn't know then that forever after, when the Vienna Waltz played, or when a travel brochure lauded the beauty of the Danube, or when this city or country was mentioned for any reason, my mind would superimpose a scene from memory of a leaping maniac yelling himself hoarse at the sight of the ghott fer dompta shvine-hoondt Amerikonisher terror fliegers.

Our lead guard reverted to quiet and cautious observance of our behavior immediately after his monologue in Vienna. It wasn't difficult to look at the ground and look tired as he had ordered; we were in our sixth day and had eaten only the cabbage water in the Ljubljana jail. But it was becoming difficult to watch our guards make and eat sandwiches from the bread and sausage they carried in their canisters.

On a train the next afternoon, our leader asked what the symbols on our shoulders were intended to mean. We shrugged because they were merely the general insignia for our air force, with feathered wings curving upward in the circle. "It has no special meaning to you?" he queried skeptically. We shrugged again. "Looks a little like butterfly," he suggested carefully. We agreed. "Iss not dangerous?" he chuckled. Unable to see reasons for his questioning, we agreed and shrugged again.

After a long silence he said, "You are lucky. Some time back, a crew like you vas picked up too. Their plane vas named 'Murder Incorporated.' It did not go so vel vit them. They got vot they stood for."

Now we understood; he was being cautious because of stories he had heard. He proved to be a persevering trip manager, able to keep us moving through the bomb-crippled areas of southern Germany.

At the next town, where road damage interrupted our travel, he went into the station and returned with a half-canteen-cup of barley soup for us. We agreed we would each take two large gulps on the first pass around; then, depending on how much was left, a small swallow or sip on another pass.

I recorded a coded version of our trip on a cigarette pack wrapper some weeks later in the permanent prison camp. The record showed we had traveled over 450 miles in the two days and three nights after leaving Vienna. Approximately half of that time was spent riding with public transport systems, mostly on railroads. The average progress while riding was less than fifteen miles per hour because of detours and delays for repairs to rails or equipment.

Over a dozen changes in travel plans were due to "allas kaput" destruction on our intended route. One-fourth of the sixty hours was spent waiting for information about conditions ahead or for alternate means of transport. And we walked the remaining fourth of the time. Walks were typically short hikes to bypass road damage, but they accumulated to over forty miles in the total trip.

As we traveled west, systems and habits of the people seemed more like the ones back home than those we had seen toward the south and east. But these systems had been converted from convenience to survival: loudspeakers in rail depots of American cities had typically announced, "Attention . . . now loading on track 29 for Joliet, Bloomington, Springfield, St. Louis. . . ." In depots here, we heard, "Achtoong, achtoong. Tsvy hoondert Amerikonisher terror fliegers, fimf undt fairtsic kilometers on norden. . . ."

The first large city after leaving Vienna was named "Munchen." We were now more able to convert German to our understanding and soon confirmed that it was Munich. In the predawn hours of the next day we reached Augsburg. Many months later, when the stories of Nazi inhumanities and mass murders in death camps circulated, I found we had passed that night within five miles of Dachau, the internment camp where more than thirty thousand humans perished.

We sprinted across a rail yard and vaulted into the side door of a slowly leaving boxcar when our leader learned that it would be the only transportation available. The car was filled with a mixed group that was apparently going to or returning from an outing together. They were in a jovial mood as they drank from their various liquor containers. After questioning our guards, they made several jeering remarks and then sang anti-enemy songs. One that they seemed to particularly enjoy included the names of Roosevelt, Churchill, and Stalin.

I remembered a similar ditty of several verses in the States where, if someone put a nickel in the juke box, a bar crowd would sing along with the chorus:

> Iss vee nix der master race?
> Ya, vee iss der master race.
> Undt zen vee "Heil, ppffft, Heil, ppffft,"
> Right in der Fuhrer's face.

I wondered why I had been surprised initially that they had a version for their purpose. And, recalling Vienna, I hoped that the ride would end before joviality turned to hostility.

Many people remember the name Nuremberg mostly because the postwar trials of notorious Nazi war criminals were held there. I remember it mostly because a young German soldier spat rapidly into my face three times as he left a train we were boarding. Our lead guard had aligned us along a railing so we could enter immediately after the passengers exited. Fortunately, the soldier's hands were occupied with luggage and the crowd was pushing him along when he recognized my insignia. As he passed me, he noticed there was a row of us and then made the same gestures at each of the other seven.

One of the guards brought us another half-cup of soup at the next stop. We agreed there should be enough for two large gulps on the first pass around. The tail gunner tipped it up and kept gulping while we stood astonished. He looked into the empty cup and became sadly remorseful. During his apologies, we reassured him that it could have happened to any one of us, that we fully believed it had not been his intent, and that we knew he couldn't help it. He repented over and over again as we left the area, until someone snarled, "Now forget it, damn it, so the rest of us can."

The guards' attitudes toward us continued to improve as it became more apparent they would complete their assignment. They were almost friendly by the third night. Though always the enemy, they now seemed like an odd form of security. We learned that they could all understand English and that another of them spoke it quite well.

On an "eight kilometer" walk over a snow-covered road in midnight moonlight, the leader urged us to increase our pace to assure arrival at the next town in time for a scheduled train. The other English-speaker suggested our shuffle could be stepped up if we sang a marching song and kept a cadence. They all agreed to being very curious to hear what American march music sounded like. When we declined to sing, the leader said somewhat jokingly that he would change the request to an order if necessary.

Memories were faded because it was well over a year since we had sung a cadence in basic training. Someone finally remembered "I've Been Working on the Railroad." The Germans chuckled during the first lines and roared hilariously at the finish. They explained they were laughing at us, not as humans but as military, because we didn't look, sound, or act like soldiers.

The guards then suggested that we hear what they had been taught and we marched to a variety of their martial music. Lines like "Doytchlandt uber allas" revolted me, but the pace was livelier. They were healthy and happy while we were starved, weary, and depressed; we had made a poor choice for our march cadence, but undeniably their music was more militarily inspiriting.

Damage became noticeably more extensive as we traveled northwest through cities within reach of British and American air forces based in England. We were impressed by the huge latticework arch that provided a transparent roof over an area the size of a football field at the rail station in Frankfurt-am-Main; and we were awed that not one of the thousands of glass panels in the latticed framework had remained unbroken by shock waves from bombings in the area.

Our guards informed us we were near our destination and watched us from nearby seats while the leader left to seek final instructions. An elderly German civilian introduced himself with fluent English after permission from the guards. He said he had lived in the States and just wanted to exchange a few feelings about the war. Because of our distrust, we politely declined.

He remained friendly, saying he understood our reluctance regardless of whether it was due to fear or hatred. He confirmed what our Nazi interrogator had told us in Ljubljana, that a major offensive had been successfully launched toward the west a week earlier. However, he added, it was now faltering into what would soon become a last-gasp effort.

He said we were far luckier than they because we would soon return to a rich country while they, with nothing, would have to try to rebuild from wreckage.

There were rumors, he confided, that Hitler had become insane, that someone from his own staff had tried to assassinate him. This attempt was too late, he regretted, to help the German people, because no one could now distinguish a Nazi from a traditional German.

Our leader returned to say that we would walk the remaining kilometers to Oberursel.

Suddenly, we turned into a gate, passed through several doors with locks, and entered a room full of German military personnel and other American captives. There was brief and terse communication with our lead guard while I was directed toward another door. I then realized that the five guards we were learning to trust had vanished and my crew mates were being pushed into other lines.

Someone said, "Dis vee take," as he removed the wristwatch I had been issued after becoming a radio operator. He muttered numbers to a man at a desk who scribbled on a slip of paper he handed to me, saying, "Iss receipt for mealitary ekveepment; your vatch."

Another goon fingered through my pockets and pulled out the square section I had cut from my parachute in Slovenia. "Dis vee keep," he said as he tossed it onto a pile behind his desk. "My handkerchief," I protested pointing, "I need it when I have a cold." He chuckled and waved me on. "A souvenir," I begged desperately; he chuckled again as another guard pulled my arm to lead me down a hallway.

"Where are we going?" I asked. "Hah," the guard snorted, "To vot you say 'solitary confinement.' " We stopped in front of a door numbered 88. He opened it, pushed me forward, pointed to a little cord beside the door and said, "Pool dis eef you need batroom," as the lock latched behind me.

My cell was the size of a small bathroom. A shelf-type cot with a thin, stiff pad and a blanket occupied one wall. There was just enough room beside the cot to pace from the door to the outside wall. Daylight came in through a slotted window below the ceiling that was too high to give a view of the local world.

I felt betrayed. I had believed that solitary confinement was used only as a punishment. I started reviewing what had happened, everything back to the mission on the sixteenth of December. Details and sequences kept coming back over and over again. Every item remained in memory in vivid detail.

Possibly several hours had passed — or had it only been minutes? If it had been only minutes, I would need something more than recirculation of recent memories to pass the time.

This would be worse than the Ljubljana jail. Here I would have to depend totally on my own mind. Perhaps this would be temporary. I could hear distant explosions, bombing. Perhaps I would be here until the end of the war — or until the end of my life.

I felt a need for orientation to something. I was not sure of bearings, because the cold winter skies had remained clouded, but I remembered we were to continue westerly out of Frankfurt. Reviewing all turns since the railroad station, I concluded my cell window faced east. I could confirm or correct that later, on a day when the sun was shining.

I knew it was the twenty-third of December. The only thing in my pockets was the "receipt" for my watch, so I made a crease with my thumbnail in a selected spot on the wooden side wall to record my first day. It was comforting to know I would have an orientation to time and direction.

After a clatter of a key in the lock, the door opened, a hand flicked in and out, the door was relatched, and a slice of black bread rolled to a stop on my cot. I had eaten only four cups of cabbage water and two gulps of barley soup in the past eight days; I would now slowly and gratefully cherish what I assumed was "lunch."

As the hours passed, I became more curious about the cord the guard said I could pull if I needed "batroom." An estimated half-hour after I pulled the cord, a different guard opened the door and locked me in a tiny latrine down the hall for another half-hour. When he returned and asked, "Vot cell?" I said, "Ocht undt ochtsic." He enjoyed my answer. Though brief, the outing had served as a change of scene.

Hours later, I was taken to a small, drab office in another part of the building, where a noncommissioned officer in his seventies gestured toward the chair across from his desk and said. "Sit. Dis iss interrogation." When I said I had already been interrogated, he sneered, "Dat vas initial. Dis iss official. Dis iss vot you ver brought here for."

He appeared very tired or despondent as he shuffled papers while confirming my name, rank, and serial number. Then:

"Vot base vas you at in Italy?"

"Orders from my government do not allow me to give information beyond what we have already confirmed."

"Vot name did your commanding officer have there?"

"I have no right to discuss this or anything other than my name, rank, and serial number."

He shook his head negatively and forced a snicker. "If you vill not tell me, den I vill tell you," he said as he pulled an indexed listing from a drawer. I had not remembered the name of our CO until he read it from his list. I shrugged and tried to look unemotional as I sat shocked, realizing that either one of our crew members had talked or that German Intelligence had learned, within the month after our arrival, which bomb group and bomb squadron my name had been assigned to. I doubted that anyone on the crew had talked.

The interrogator seemed smugly sure that he had impressed me regardless of my attempt to conceal a reaction. When he lifted a large card-mounted map of Italy from a slot beside his desk and then an organizational chart of the Fifteenth Air Force, he enjoyed another sneer with, "See, vee don't really need vot you say; vee yust giff you shance to talk if you vant to."

Placement of our bases on their map didn't surprise me, because Americans had taken over areas Germans had occupied and we used airstrips they had built. But I was impressed by their ability to identify details of all units and individuals in charge of them.

He then added, "Vee are still looking for your two pilots and your navigator." I hoped my astonishment wasn't apparent when he accurately identified those missing. Having captured eight crewmen, they should have been looking for only two more from a normal ten-man crew; the addition of a photographer to our plane hadn't confused German Intelligence.

If their information had merely come from prior crew listings, they would have been looking for Sandy and Ronnie. Because this was our initial mission, Ronnie remained unassigned at the base, and Cord, whom we had just met the morning of the mission, flew as first pilot. This meant the Germans had acquired this information within eight days.

I still didn't mistrust any of our group. I wondered, however, if American Military Intelligence was this fast and accurate. It was no longer surprising that the Germans could have the massive numbers of rail-mounted antiaircraft guns at the right target before our planes got there.

The interrogator added, "Your pilots and navigator vill not be as lucky as you. Our people are sick undt tired of being bombed undt harassed by you every day; dey vill not treat dem so vell."

He pushed a button to beckon a guard. And he managed another sneer as he concluded, "But den, vot iss luck? Tomorrow, your people vill celebrate Christmas Eve, undt dey vont care about you, because dey vont know ver you are, undt dey don't know vot var iss like."

He was mostly right. Six months later when I arrived home, I learned that a "Missing in Action" telegram hadn't been received until the third of January, eleven days after the interrogator's final sneer; my people wanted to hear only about selected parts of the war; and they wanted to believe that, because I was so very young, perhaps I had misinterpreted some of the feelings that I thought I had detected.

I found my cell to be icy cold after the guard latched the door behind me again. Apparently the interrogator's section of the building was partially heated. The day had been cold, and a more frigid air mass moving into the area was rapidly dropping the temperature as daylight faded. I knew I wouldn't be able to sleep. I felt I should do physical exercises later in the evening and wondered, considering the starvation intake, how to best conserve calories.

After odd noises in the hallway, my door swung open and a guard directed me to join a line of other prisoners who were being brought out of their cells. We were taken past a window where a goon gave us each three thin gray blankets.

The line then continued into a new addition of the building. It was colder. The recently cut lumber was white with a thick coating of hoarfrost. Wind whistled through spaces between the boards of the outside walls.

We were locked into rooms in groups of six, where we were to sleep in pairs on three wide wooden shelves nailed against the outside wall. Through chattering teeth, we discussed, not how to sleep, but how to avoid freezing to death.

The door opened with new instructions to leave the blankets and follow the crowd to a large room where word spread that we were the lucky ones who would leave in the morning because our "processing" was complete.

There was a small woodburning stove at one end of the stark room; and there were three hundred airmen, mostly Americans and a few British. The instant sociability was exhilarating and the comradeship was comforting. It reassured us that we were still trying to be brave soldiers in spite of some obvious misfortunes. We had all learned how to appreciate the moment; freezing or starving could be worried about later.

I met two of my crew members. Their surprise at the Germans' accurate and timely Intelligence data had been similar to mine; they also felt it hadn't come from our group. One said, "Remember that 'No capeesh, no capeesh' line the Eye-ties always gave us back at the base. They capeeshed everything and radioed it straight to Berlin."

There were various types, shapes, and sizes of splints and bandages in the room; the most frightening one made one man's head look like a huge marshmallow. From the man's back, one noticed he was wearing only the scorched lining from his flight jacket, because all the outer fabric had burned off except two straps that flapped loosely where they had been protected from the fire by his chute harness. From the front, there was a little triangular window in the marshmallow, with eyes in the upper corners and a mouth in the lower corner. Except for red scales and scabs, it was the same smiling face of Lieutenant Miligan that had greeted us as he tripped the hand-counter at all of those meals on the *David G. Farragut* two months earlier.

He still had good words for everybody, because he felt he had been saved by an odd miracle: everything in his plane was on fire after attacks by Jerry fighters; he finally found a hatch, dove into the outside wind and, when the chute popped him to a stop, the flames burning his clothes blew out!

Many conversations around the group reviewed relationships with lost friends from former training schools and stations. After overhearing the familiar name Weslauski, I listened more closely to another story being told about a fire that caused a jump — but without a chute. Hardly daring to question, I asked, "Did he take Basic at Keesler? Was his first name . . .? Was he from the little town of . . .? After "Yes" to all questions, the speaker asked, "Where did you know him from?" and I answered, "Keesler."

I knew a brave soldier doesn't cry; he rocks his lower molars against the uppers to control emotions while he walks to the stove pretending interest in how it's constructed. When someone says, "Jees, you sure hear some weird stories around this place," the soldier tests his voice with, "Ya." If that sounds steady, he adds, "You sure do." When he's sure his speech is firm, he continues:

"I just heard my bunk buddy from Basic was last seen as a screaming bonfire, running without a chute through a big hole the Jerries blew in the side of his ship. He came shrieking through the bomb bay into the waist and kept running when he saw the opening. They said a chute couldn't have opened anyway because they were only a few hundred feet off the ground. They crash landed in the next mile. Some of them made it. A couple of them are here.

"He was a quiet, thoughtful type — one of the finest I had met; a little afraid of facing combat — like, who wasn't?

"Last year on Sunday mornings, before the sergeants came through for a work detail, he and I sat across bunks from each other and talked about the best ways to get back into civilian life after the war is over. We promised to look each other up. At least, I know what he'll be doing if this war is ever over.

"Remember that line in our song 'We live in fame or go down in flame?' He sure never got to be very famous. Some just get to do the last part, I guess."

Then it was time for another walk — because it was time to rock the molars again.

Barracks at Basic Training, Keesler Field, Biloxi, Mississippi. (From USAAF Service brochure/catalog purchased at Keesler Field in 1943)

Pvt. Melvin G. TenHaken, who was inducted on July 10, this year, has been assigned to the Technical School, Army Air Forces Training Command, Sioux Falls, S. D., for training as a radio operator-mechanic. When he has completed his 20-week course, he will be fully trained to take his place as a member of a highly skilled bomber crew of the army air forces. He is a graduate of Oostburg High school, this year, and his parents are Mr. and Mrs. Gerrit Ten Haken, Jr., Oostburg. He was formerly at Camp Grant, Ill., and Kessler Field, Miss.

Clip from "Heroes in the Service" section of *The Sheboygan* (Wis.) *Press*, 2 Dec. 1943. (Courtesy, *The Sheboygan* Press)

Graduation photo from Radio Operator/Mechanic School, Sioux Falls, South Dakota. (Photo, USAAF)

A family photo taken at the author's parents' home on his last furlough before shipping overseas.

bers. The fourth brother, A/S Robert Lubbers, is receiving boot training at Great Lakes, Ill.

Pvt. Lubbers is the niece of Irwin J. Lubbers, president of Central college, Pella, Iowa, writer and lecturer on India and educational administration.

Davis-Monthan Field, Tucson, Ariz. — Corp. Melvin G. Ten Haken, 20, son of Mr. and Mrs. Gerrit Ten Haken, box 174, Oostburg, was recently graduated from this combat crew training school and will soon go to an overseas combat zone for active duty as a radio operator on a B-24 Liberator bomber.

Corp. Ten Haken, who entered the service in July, 1943, is a member of a 10-man aerial team that has been welded into fighting shape in a two and one-half months' training program here which included practice bombing, aerial gunnery, simulated contact with enemy aircraft, long-range navigational flights and emergency landing procedures.

He is a graduate of Oostburg High school in the class of 1943.

Big Spring, Tex. — According to an announcement from the office of Col. Ralph C. Rockwood, commanding officer of the army air forces bombardier school, Big Spring, Tex., Ronald J. Stillwell, son of Albert Stillwell of 1534 St. Clair avenue, Sheboygan, has arrived at this school to receive his pre-cadet training. Most of the time spent here will be on the line where he will be instructed in the basic fundamentals of airplane maintenance and operation, which includes a general knowledge of radio, armament, flight theory and aircraft mechanics.

The Bushmen, a race of short, yellowish-brown nomad hunters, are believed to be the earliest human inhabitants of south Africa of whom there is any reliable historical record.

Clip from "Heroes in the Service" section of *The Sheboygan* (Wis.) *Press*, 21 Sept. 1944. (Courtesy *The Sheboygan Press*)

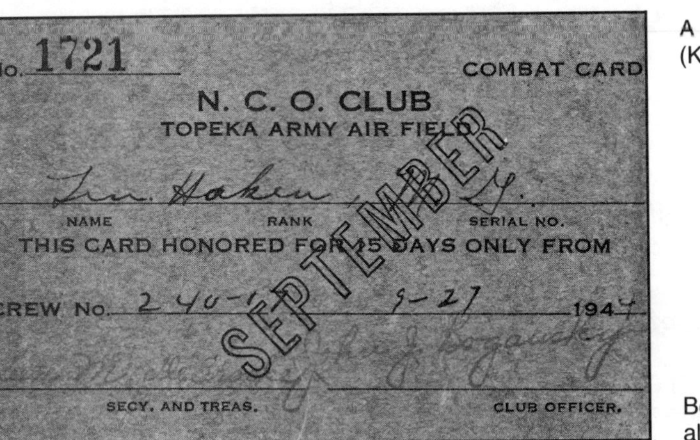

No. 1721 COMBAT CARD

N. C. O. CLUB

TOPEKA ARMY AIR FIELD

SEPTEMBER

NAME RANK SERIAL NO.

THIS CARD HONORED FOR 15 DAYS ONLY FROM

CREW No. 2 40-1 9-27 1947

SECY. AND TREAS. CLUB OFFICER.

A copy of the Service Club card for use at Topeka Army Air Field (Kansas) while there.

Below: Assembling a convoy of American ships. (Courtesy, National Archives)

Technical School

Army Air Forces Central Technical Training Command

SIOUX FALLS, SOUTH DAKOTA

This is to certify that

Pvt. TenHaken, Melvin G. 36826670 811th TSS

has fired the qualification course, dismounted, with the

U. S. AUTOMATIC PISTOL, CALIBER 45, M1911A1

and has qualified as

Expert

DATE 14 April 1944

SCORE 86.6%

JOHN OLESZCZUK
Captain, Air Corps
Director, Small Arms Training.

A copy of the certificate for Expert classification with U.S. Automatic Pistol, Cal. 45.(badge below).

Right: Photo of German Kgf identification card.

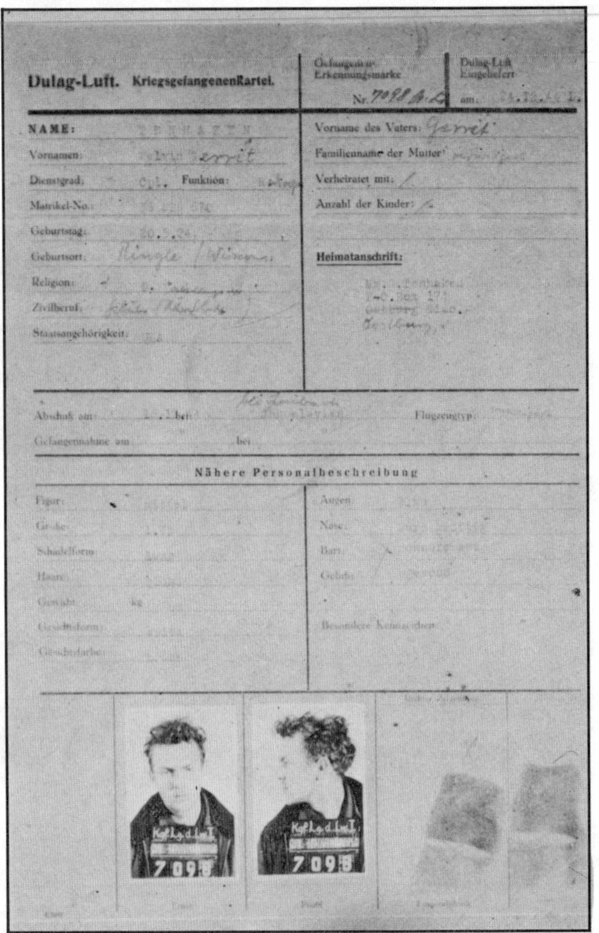

Dulag-Luft. Kriegsgefangenenkartei.

Gefangenen-Erkennungsmarke Nr. 7098 [illegible]

Dulag-Luft Eingeliefert am: [illegible]

NAME: [illegible]

Vornamen: [illegible] Gerrit

Dienstgrad: Cpl. Funktion: [illegible]

Matrikel-No.: [illegible]

Geburtstag: 20.5.24.

Geburtsort: Ringle [illegible]

Religion: [illegible]

Zivilberuf: [illegible]

Staatsangehörigkeit: [illegible]

Vorname des Vaters: Gerrit

Familienname der Mutter: [illegible]

Verheiratet mit: /

Anzahl der Kinder: /

Heimatanschrift:

Abschuß am: [illegible] bei: [illegible] Flugzeugtyp: [illegible]

Gefangennahme am: bei:

Nähere Personalbeschreibung

Figur:

Größe:

Schädelform:

Haare:

Gewicht: kg

Gesichtsform:

Gesichtsfarbe:

Augen:

Nase:

Bart:

Gebiß:

Besondere Kennzeichen:

Kgf. Lg. d. Lw. I 7098

"Moon-yea Eye-tal-yon."

CLASS OF SERVICE

This is a full-rate Telegram or Cablegram unless its deferred character is indicated by a suitable symbol above or preceding the address.

WESTERN UNION

1204

A. N. WILLIAMS, PRESIDENT — NEWCOMB CARLTON, CHAIRMAN OF THE BOARD — J. C. WILLEVER, FIRST VICE-PRESIDENT

SYMBOLS

DL=Day Letter
NT=Overnight Telegram
LC=Deferred Cable
NLT=Cable Night Letter
Ship Radiogram

The filing time shown in the date line on telegrams and day letters is STANDARD TIME at point of origin. Time of receipt is STANDARD TIME at point of destination

730 AM JA 52 Govt 10 extra Attempt to deliver from Sheboygan unsuccessful unable contact relatives

WUX Washington DC 8:00PM 1-2-45

Mrs Anna Ten Haken
Oostburg Wis

The Secretary of War desires me to express his deep regret that your son Corporal Melvin G. Ten Haken has been reported missing in action since sixteen December over Italy. If further details or other information are received you will be promptly notified

Dunlop, Acting
The Adjutant General

THE COMPANY WILL APPRECIATE SUGGESTIONS FROM ITS PATRONS CONCERNING ITS SERVICE

The "missing in action" telegram received by the author's mother on 3 January 1945.

FIFTEENTH AIR FORCE
Office of the Commanding General
A.P.O. 520

2 January 1945

Mrs. Anna TenHaken
Oostburg, Wisconsin

My dear Mrs. TenHaken:

The Liberator on which your son, Corporal Melvin G. TenHaken, 36826670, participated as the ~~top turret~~ radio gunner, failed to return from a combat mission to Brux, Czechoslovakia on December 16, 1944. Since that date, Melvin and his crew have been missing in action.

Returning airmen report that his ship fell from formation in the vicinity of Trieste, Italy, on the return flight from the target. Before the bomber entered the undercast below, seven parachutes were seen to emerge. It is very possible that the remainder of the crew were able to bail out after the plane passed from sight. Should word be received in the future the War Department will notify you at once.

Melvin's personal belongings have been assembled for shipment to the Effects Quartermaster, Army Effects Bureau, Kansas City, Missouri, who will in turn forward them to the designated beneficiary.

Without the contributions made by men like your son, victory would be an impossibility. You may be sure that Melvin's record of service speaks highly of the valuable contribution he has made to the struggle that engages us all at this time.

Very sincerely yours,

N F Twining

N. F. TWINING
Major General, USA
Commanding

The letter forwarded by the War Department several days after the "missing in action" telegram.

Cpl. Melvin Ten Haken of Oostburg has been reported missing in action over Italy since December 16. He was a radio gunner aboard a B-24 Liberator.

A copy of a clip from *The Sheboygan* (Wis.) *Press*, 6 Jan. 1945. (Courtesy, *The Sheboygan Press*)

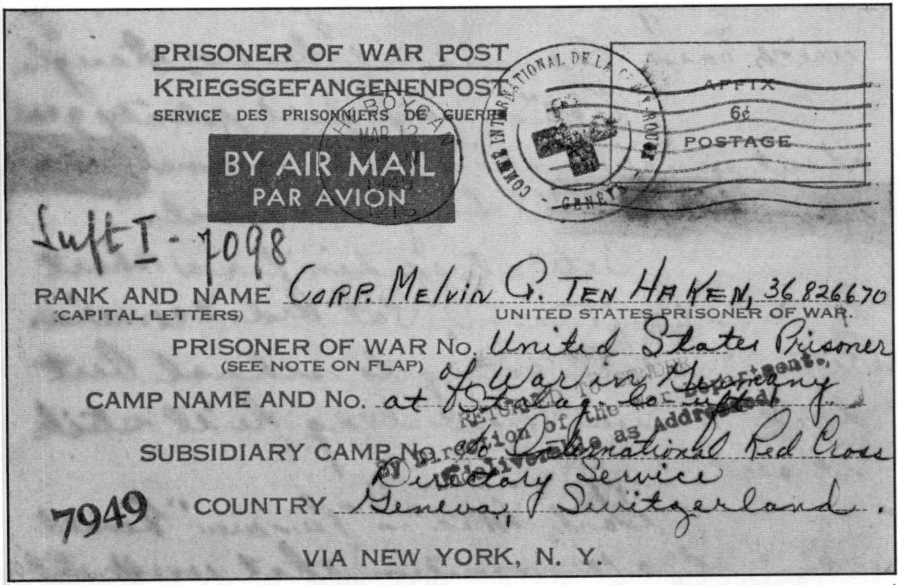
PRISONER OF WAR POST
KRIEGSGEFANGENENPOST
SERVICE DES PRISONNIERS DE GUERRE
BY AIR MAIL
PAR AVION
AFFIX 6¢ POSTAGE
Luft I - 7098
RANK AND NAME (CAPITAL LETTERS) Corp. Melvin G. Ten Haken, 36826670
UNITED STATES PRISONER OF WAR.
PRISONER OF WAR No. (SEE NOTE ON FLAP) United States Prisoner of War in Germany
CAMP NAME AND No. at Stalag Luft I
SUBSIDIARY CAMP No. c/o International Red Cross Directory Service
7949 COUNTRY Geneva, Switzerland.
VIA NEW YORK, N. Y.

One of the many letters returned by the Service with other personal items several weeks after liberation.

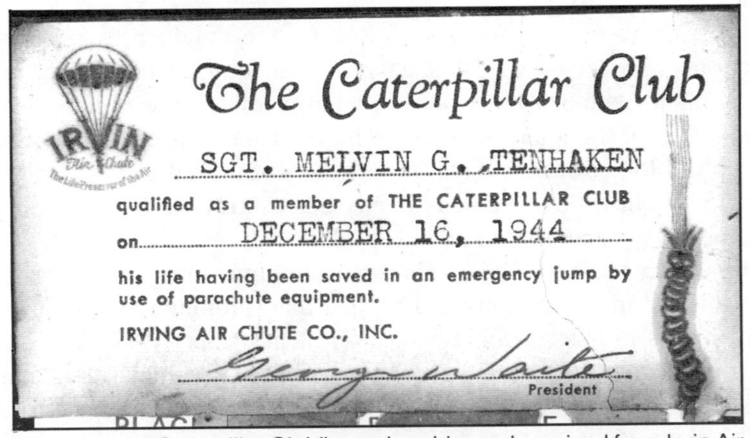

The Caterpillar Club
SGT. MELVIN G. TENHAKEN
qualified as a member of THE CATERPILLAR CLUB
on DECEMBER 16, 1944
his life having been saved in an emergency jump by use of parachute equipment.
IRVING AIR CHUTE CO., INC.
George Waite
President

The author's "Caterpillar Club" membership card received from Irvin Air Chute a few months after liberation.

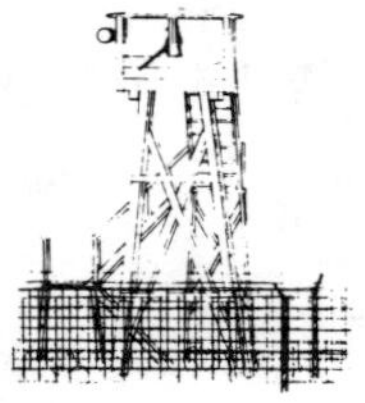

Chapter 9

Beer in Berlin on New Year's Eve

The din of conversation among three hundred prisoners in the large room after solitary confinement was suddenly quieted for an announcement. A British "leftenant" introduced himself to say German guards had asked him to speak for them.

He said the temperature outside was still dropping and the guards wondered if we would prefer to remain in that room to sleep rather than return to the cells. After an immediate murmur of approval, he added that we would be permitted to keep our belts and shoes in return for a pledge to not attempt an escape. The crowd's initial reaction to that was a round of bewildered chuckles.

The guards were obviously perturbed by the laughter. After terse new instructions were given to the speaker, he announced that this was not a laughing matter; either there would be an immediate show of hands supporting the pledge, or shoes and belts would be piled in the hall. After pledging, we were allowed to get our blankets from the frost-covered rooms.

The fire in our little stove had already burned out and it became apparent that the best way to conserve heat was to share it, so everybody took a partner. Mine was from southern California and jestingly assumed I would be better able to tolerate the cold than he. I argued that, although we had had many subzero nights in Wisconsin, I had never slept on the floor of an unheated garage during one. We selected a position to favor my aching shoulder and the floor was soon covered with pairs of back-to-back airmen wrapped in cocoons of six blankets each.

In the morning, we took a freezing march to a train of coaches waiting to take us forty miles north to Wetzlar. Another pledge was required after we had boarded as an alternative to having our belts and shoes piled at the end of the car. This time there were no chuckles.

After ten miles en route, riders with window seats quietly nudged partners to point out huge flights of bombers heading east high in the sunny sky. These were comrades-in-arms from the Eighth Air Force in England. We suppressed our urge to cheer for their freedom and their mission as guards watched from the ends of the car.

Various types of American fighter planes soon entered the area. These noticeably worried the Germans, who studied directions of their flight patterns with obvious concern. Our train slowed to a stop, excited messages were exchanged between train engineers and guards, and finally came an announcement: We would be locked in the cars while they would retreat to an opening under the overhang of a low embankment a short block to our right. They assured us they had adequate fire power to put anyone down who got up from a seat.

We heard the doors being locked, saw the guards run, and watched them cowering under their little cave-like cover. The fighter planes strafed targets around the area, but, though we were in clear view in an open space, none came near us. That must have been at least partly because Americans didn't casually and normally strafe civilian trains of passenger coaches, as had been implied by many among our enemies.

When all was clear an hour later, the guard crew returned and the trip continued. The prison camp, on a windswept plain near Wetzlar, was an enclosure of barbed wire surrounding wooden barracks. It was called Dulag Luft, which we soon learned meant "temporary" camp for airmen. There were many hundreds of Americans and some British waiting here for the time to pass until they would be "moved on."

Most of the remainder of our first day was spent "processing," which meant standing in line while German clerks verified our identification and the area or direction from which we had been brought into camp.

Myers, the crew's nose gunner, suddenly appeared in one of the processing areas, and we agreed to try to stay together. Though it was increasingly difficult to maintain a cheerful outlook, it was comforting to be in a group of our own kind and at least part of the time out of sight of armed guards.

After being assigned to a barrack, we waited again in another area before being taken to a room. Here we heard encouraging news from internees who had been in the camp for days and weeks: we would eat — probably the following day! The Red Cross provided food parcels with dry and canned foods and cigarettes; contents were carefully audited and sparingly meted out, they said, but the food would probably be better than anything since our first day of captivity.

As we entered the room, we found sleeping facilities again to be board shelves with one blanket for each sleeper, but there was a pack of cigarettes on every blanket. These packs had been placed there by American prisoners who knew we would be as delighted as they had been in a similar situation. This was an era when cigarettes were not yet considered a hazard to health but rather as one of life's little pleasures, and most nonsmokers learned to use the little pleasures as a way to pass the time as prisoners.

I claimed the bunk above mine for Myers and noticed that he slipped his cigarette pack into a pocket when he arrived, as I had mine. Then he turned and said, "You know, this may seem silly, but this is Christmas Eve — "

"Yes, I do know," I responded. "I haven't been able to decide if I want to think about that or try to ignore it."

"Well, I was wondering; when you were a kid, did you open your presents on Christmas Eve or Christmas morning?" he asked with an embarrassed smile.

"Christmas morning. Why?"

"Well, we did too, and — this may be a little silly — but I was wondering if you'd like to exchange Christmas presents in the morning."

"I think it's a great idea. It's not at all silly. What do we have to do that's better?"

The outside cold was less severe that night and there was some heat in the building.

Everyone was awake after the first person moved in the morning. Some said, "Merry Christmas," as they sat up. No one had a comb or a toothbrush and the new day started where the previous one ended — with nothing to do. Some just sat and stared blank-faced into space; and some sadly reminisced about things they had done as children on Christmas.

Myers and I faced each other with forced smiles and a hushed, "Merry Christmas, I have a little something for you." We then extended hands, saying, "I'm sorry I didn't have any thing to wrap it with," as we exchanged packs of cigarettes. After opening our presents, we enjoyed one of "life's little pleasures" while exchanging comments:

"Maybe that was silly, but I think it made me feel better."

"I don't think it was silly. I'm sure it made me feel better."

We questioned whether we could have given the present without the assurance of receiving an identical one in return; and we agreed we'd sooner discuss that some other time.

An invitation to a Christmas dinner later in the day was hard to believe, but we went to a large room where tables were already set with plates of food! There were no tablecloths or napkins; only bare essentials on rough boards in a stark room. But to those who had had little or nothing in days or weeks, the spread looked almost elegant, more like a dining room than a mess hall. Despite miniscule portions by average standards, there was variety: a tiny piece of Spam, a hard graham-type cracker, a piece of black bread, and even a bit of hard chocolate from a D-bar. It was almost filling to shrunken stomachs, temporarily. As with the cigarettes, we knew this wasn't from the Germans, except for the bread. Plates had been prepared by American prisoner staff, but the Germans had permitted it. Everything we were experiencing helped our morale.

A request for quiet in the room brought a speaker from among those who had helped with the preparation. He "welcomed" us to Dulag Luft with a "Merry Christmas," while German guards at the rear watched and nervously readjusted and repositioned the shoulder slings of their Mauser rifles. And he informed us that this meal had been better than typical because this was a special day, particularly for the newcomers.

He then led the group in singing "Silent Night" and a first verse and chorus of a few other best-known Christmas hymns and carols. No one could cry because we were all brave soldiers, but many used a finger tip to occasionally relieve an itch from high on a cheek.

The following morning we learned that the German word "appel" meant "roll call." We stood in formations in the snow and shivered, grouped according to sleeping areas, while goons counted, questioned each other, recounted, questioned again, recounted and reconfirmed seemingly endlessly.

We witnessed a sight each morning during roll call which was then still quite new to the world. The vapor trail of an unmanned rocket would appear several thousand feet above a launching site some miles west of us and form a huge arc high in the sky toward London, four hundred miles farther west.

We called the rockets V1's until corrected by a rumor that these were now a revised version that Germany called V2. The Third Reich was no longer able to fuel an effective force of fighter planes, but the rocket development reportedly carried a special approval from Hitler; as with the flame-throwers on his tanks earlier, he supposedly derived a diabolical glee from terrorizing opposition with weapons they didn't have and had no defense against.

Our appreciation for efforts of the Red Cross and the YMCA was further enhanced on the day after Christmas, when we were walked to a stockroom to be issued items that had fittingly been dubbed "joy boxes." Each new prisoner received one box containing a toothbrush, toothpaste, a small sewing kit, two large white handkerchiefs, two pairs of socks, a hand-knit sweater, and a set of underwear. We were encouraged when we heard the Germans were allowing an occasional, though rare, visit by the International Red Cross to organized American prisoner-of-war camps.

Contents of the joy boxes varied slightly because they were made up from donated materials. Most sizes were medium, and some trading among recipients was necessary to correct problems with fit. Colors of the sweaters had been the choice of "the woman behind the man behind the gun"; some of us wondered if she would have worked as enthusiastically if she had known it would go to a man behind barbed wire.

Three days later, German guards suddenly entered to tell us to follow the leader; we were being moved out of the camp. A train of passenger coaches took more than two hundred of us north out of Wetzlar. Myers and I had tried to stay together but had become hopelessly separated during boarding.

The cars contained compartments which, in better days, had been designed to seat four; two couples facing each other. Six of us were wedged into each compartment for the next five days. The severe crowding necessitated sitting erect while asleep or awake.

I had a window seat. Rough boards had been nailed across all windows, but an eighth-inch space between boards at eye level permitted a horizontally slotted view of the outside world, and a one-inch diameter knothole in the board above allowed telescopic study of given scenes. With this seat came the responsibility for occasional reports of outside activities to others in the compartment.

We were heading into central Germany. After passing through Kassel the first day, our course turned northeast toward Berlin. Interestingly, this part of the country dealt with the devastation of air attacks differently from the less populous areas in the southeast. There, after a bombing, alternate means of transport were used until repair crews could be brought in. Here, within reach of England, they had been hit by American "Heavies" and "Mediums" and fighter-bombers daily, and by Britain's Royal Air Force nightly, over a much longer period; and they had learned to keep repair crews working continuously.

The repairmen were prisoners of war from other countries; I noticed the "Kgf" painted on the backs and trouser legs of their clothing. When our new guards became more trusting and talkative, they explained that Kgf was an abbreviation for "kriegsgefangenen," meaning war prisoner. The workers were "mostly Russian" but also "many French," they said.

Unlike our trip west from Vienna, on which we walked to other transportation, here the same distance took twice the time because we waited for hours in the railcars during repairs.

Some scenes were difficult to comprehend as I peered through my knothole. A crater, caused by a bomb that had blown away six railroad tracks in a second, was being repaired by dozens of prisoners with pickaxes and shovels. I tried to analyze the sequence and variety of forces that had changed a straight steel rail into a full turn of a gigantic corkscrew that protruded from the earth to a second-story level. But the emaciated and demoralized workers were concerned only with how to uproot and replace it.

I was initially surprised by a basic behavior that was different from anything I had seen: workers and guards in the rail yards looked in another direction while passengers from trains, both men and women, picked places among the rubble to urinate or defecate. Public plumbing was sometimes stopped by bombings, but biology continued for survivors fortunate enough to imbibe and ingest.

I remembered the drunken suggestions from revelers in the Two Hearts Cafe near home about what we had to do to "the damn Germans to end the damn war." We had done it; it wasn't that easy.

I remembered the excited monologue of our lead guard behind the bushes in Vienna when he said, "Vee treat you Americans better than other prisoners . . . vee are hit harder by you than anybody ever before. . . ." The destruction here in this phase of the war was being caused by Americans and Britons. Yet the Russians, whom the Germans loathed, and the French, whom they detested, were being worked to death to fix it while we sat and watched through knotholes. The German military had an odd respect for us largely because our country could continue dropping evidence of strength into their country. It was chilling to know that we would be the ones nudged with rifle butts and probed with bayonets if our country's show of strength ever faltered.

We traveled through Magdeburg on our second day. During one of the delays there, our guards brought canteen cups of soup from the rail station. We passed the cup for our compartment around the one-swallow-per-turn circuit among the six of us.

Everyone felt something significant should happen on the third day because it was the last day of the year. Late that afternoon we rolled into the outskirts of Berlin. There were mixed emotions: was this significant or would we sooner not have come here?

The train stopped. There was the typical evidence of crumbled buildings as in any of the heavily bombed cities, but there was no sign of rail damage to cause our delay. Hours later we moved, but only several blocks to another part of the city.

Though discussion was kept to a brief hushed agreement, we were all anxious to move out. Wouldn't the Royal Air Force drop all the bombs they had available onto "Big B" at midnight? Hadn't that become the Allies' traditional way of saying "Happy New Year" to our enemy? We assumed the Germans would lock us in the train again and dash to some nearby bomb shelter.

The noise level among our guards outside the compartment increased as the last hour ticked toward midnight. A few of them were obviously starting celebrations by getting into the "spirits" of the hour, while others sternly objected to the insobriety because of the importance of their post. Our door slid open with "yust minutes to go" and a grinning guard handed in a canteen cup with, "Sherman bier, so you kon alvays say you hod hoppy Nineseen-fimf-undt-fairtsig in Bierlean mit Sherman bier."

We accepted. We needed the water in the beer and we hoped there were also a few calories as we passed the cup mimicking, "Happy New Year." Toasts for a successful year ahead seemed somewhat of a repetition of Lincoln's thoughts in the Civil War when he pondered the fact that both sides were asking the same God to help them win.

After midnight, we nervously wondered what had delayed the bombers. The train slowly started out of Berlin before morning. There had been no bombs. We assumed bad weather hung above us to the west, and we remained sure that the Germans had parked our train near a known bomb shelter.

We continued north-northeast to Stettin, near the confluence of the Oder River with the Pomeranian Gulf. This was the eastern German border area that was allotted to Poland after the war. No one in our group was sure where we were at the time and, with our defeated morale, no one cared anymore. A study of maps clarified the course of that trip months later when the Russians recaptured that area and destroyed the source of electricity for our prison camp.

We humored ourselves by calling our attitudes "compartment fever," and in the evening of the second of January we arrived at Barth, in the northern tip of Germany on the Baltic Sea, 120 miles north of Berlin. We slept for one last night wedged erect in the seats, and we walked the last long mile of this 450-mile trip in the morning.

At the end of the walk, there was another barbed-wire enclosure around shabby wooden barracks. German guards rechecked our identification during long waits in the entrance area. The name of this camp was Stalag Luft I which meant it was a "permanent" camp for air force personnel. The definition was disheartening; we preferred the "temporary" Dulag.

As at the previous camp, I noticed a familiar face excitedly trying to get my attention. It was Hartfield, our crew's tail gunner. He had seen other crew members but hadn't been able to get through to them. We agreed to try to stay together.

The longest wait here was for the completion of a summary identification card with photographs. Data that had been entered on the form at Dulag was reconfirmed and there was one last attempt by a clerk to add information to the unanswered questions.

An office-worker inked my finger tips and pressed the prints onto the card. Another informed me that my prisoner number would be 7098, as he slid the number-cards into position for a photograph. After chalking my name on the board-form he had set in front of me, he snapped a front view. He then snickered, "Undt now luke to sit undt laugh at Meekey Mouse like you do in da Shtates." Mickey's picture hung on the side wall.

Not realizing that the cartoon caricature would make a large and lasting comeback in a communication medium yet to be developed, we jested in the next waiting room at the Germans' ignorance in not knowing that "Meekey Mouse" had started to fade into oblivion "way back a couple of years" when we had still been in high school.

We also discussed whether questions like "family name of mother?" were merely asked as a way to harass or weaken us. We knew that our government allowed U.S. servicemen with an "H" for the Hebrew religion on their "dog tags" to get a reissue with a "P" for Protestant. That was because the German government was known to discriminate against Jews. But we didn't know, until months later when someone was taken from our room, that there was an obsession for removing anyone with any Jewish ancestry from among us.

At another stop someone dipped a half-inch brush into a pail of red paint to scrawl a crude "USA" on our flight jackets. The guards seemed pleased to indicate this was special treatment because it was an exception to the "Kgf" generally used to identify other prisoners of war.

Before assignment to a barrack, we went through a store room to receive our issue of bedding. Each of us was handed a burlap bag the size of a small pillowcase and another six-foot-long bag for a mattress.

I was delighted to see the next room half-full of shredded newspapers. An attendant scooped his hands into the bedding pile, compressed a wad to the size of a basketball, and shoved it into the burlap pillowcase I held open.

I quickly tucked the case under an arm and opened the mattress while he laughed boisterously saying, "Das iss allus." I didn't immediately understand and nodded toward the bedding pile while holding the mattress bag open. He mistook my ignorance for persistence and bellowed, "Rouse," as he sternly jabbed a finger toward the exit. Then I understood: they didn't care how we distributed our few shreds of bedding ration; they were annoyed only if we asked for more.

After a final issue of two gray blankets each, we were walked through occupied areas to a newer addition to the camp. Twelve of us were left in a room intended for twenty-four; the others would arrive later. Hartfield and I claimed adjacent sleeping spots on the top shelf.

The camp's title of "permanent" now began to take on meaning: we would continue existing here into an unknown, unmeasurable future.

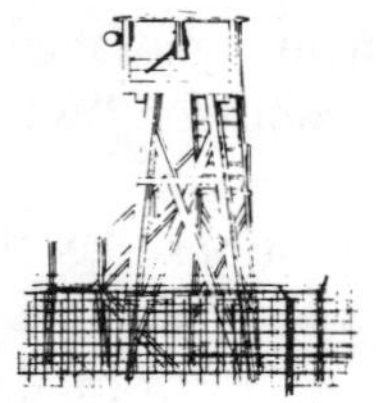

Chapter 10

The Evening Paper

Our floors were cold because they were exposed to the weather. As we tried to recall our first walk from the front gate, we knew that the barracks in the older compounds were different, but we could remember only that they were built on the ground; ours were on stilts, with floors three feet above the ground.

We hadn't cared about the reason on our first walk through because we were too depressed at the sight of what would be our "permanent" home. Explanations became obvious later: as inmates developed ways to remove floor boards and dig tunnels, the Germans built the newer barracks with visible crawl spaces below them.

Most of us on the inside learned more about the camp and the reasons for its administrative actions after the war was over than we did while imprisoned there.

Within hours after our arrival each of us was taken to an empty room for a "background quiz" by a senior prisoner. Simple questions about U.S. geography, sports, movie personalities, and other nonmilitary subjects seemed inane and caused suspicion, until the new prisoner was told he had passed an internal security check. The purpose was to prevent the Germans from slipping a spy in among us to get answers about our covert activities.

The twelve of us who had cleared the security check were taken to another empty room to be apprised of general overt rules issued by the Germans and supposedly in agreement with the Geneva Convention. First, of course, every prisoner was subordinate to any German, regardless of rank.

Internally, the Germans advocated that the highest-ranked military prisoner be administratively "in charge" of all internees; with that arrangement, they could issue one order to the internal official to be transmitted to all prisoners through his organization. That arrangement had also proved advantageous to us.

Almost eight thousand prisoners already inhabited the camp, and more were arriving at ever increasing rates. Col. Hubert Zemke, an ace fighter pilot with twenty-eight downed German planes to his credit, was the internal officer in charge of the entire impoundment.

There were four separately fenced areas called "compounds," each with roughly two thousand prisoners. There had been only a "south compound" and a "north compound" earlier in the war, but two additions were built adjacent to the north compound later; ours was called North Compound Three. Our compound leader was Colonel Gabreski, also an ace fighter pilot with twenty-eight downed German planes to his credit.

Each barrack also had a designated administrative officer, often with the rank of captain. As prisoners, we were not to worry about those mentions of rank; among us on the inside those men were just other prisoners of war.

There would be more to learn about overt administration later. Fundamental awareness of some aspects of covert activities was more important initially, the senior POW told us. A basic rule to help our internal causes, he explained, would simply be to maintain the mum attitude of "name, rank, and serial number" in any contact with Germans here.

"How might this be an advantage to us?" he said. "I'll explain." The mild flavor of American cigarettes had made them highly desirable wherever they were known; we had no money, he acknowledged, but five packs of cigarettes came in every Red Cross food parcel. Just one cigarette for every man in the camp amounted to forty cartons.

If we traded these to the right goon for something we needed, even if he smoked a carton, he could buy "a hell of a lot of carnal excitement in the drab world out there" with the other thirty-nine cartons. However, this would work only if the goon could totally trust his contact, because he would be executed by the Nazi hierarchy for any known fraternization with us for personal gain.

There would be a few among us, our informant continued, who were official traders, but to protect the system they were never called that; they were referred to as "interpreters," and we wouldn't know who they might be. The stakes were too high to ever consider personal requests for individual items.

"Now that you all know this much, forget that you've heard it," he advised, "because, like the posters in the States warned: 'A slip of the lip can sink a ship.' After you've had a chance to see what is already available, if anyone has a plausible idea later for a community-type item that might be helpful, talk to the administrative official in the barrack, because he knows all about the stuff we never talk about.

"Finally, the point of all of this is to offer evidence that something like I've just discussed is already working to our advantage," he continued. "Would you like to hear the latest scoop on how the war is progressing? I don't mean the kind of crap the Jerries would like to hope you'd believe; I mean the real truth, straight from the British Broadcasting Company, put together by our own boys here on the inside!"

Not that night, he explained, but maybe the next, as soon as the remaining twelve in our room had been "checked out," we'd start receiving the evening paper. It was called the "POW WOW."

"After the Jerries drop the bar across the outside door," he continued, "after the blackout shutters are closed, someone will knock on your door. They'll hand you a folded sheet of paper the size of a business letter. Don't ask questions; take it.

"Have a little fire going in your stove. If you hear a yell of 'Attention' or 'Enemy up' while you've got it, burn it immediately. Have your best reader ready. Cluster around as soon as you get it and have him read just loud enough so you can hear him, but not loud enough so a Jerry guard sittin' under your floor could hear what he says. When you've finished, knock on the door to your right and hand it to them."

The Germans knew we were getting better news than they were getting, but they had never discovered exactly how, and they continued running periodic searches.

There were more rules protecting survival of the paper: never question how or where it exists until after the war; in discussion of the war's progress, don't ever talk about the source of the news; in case an issue of the POW WOW doesn't arrive, don't look for reasons.

After a day of confusion and another night of troubled sleep, it was time to get acquainted with the other twenty-three inhabitants of the room. Shortly after an exchange of names, one of the new roommates started relating details of where he had bailed out and how and why. Several occupants from other rooms, who were still assisting with orientation, encircled us and started chorusing an obviously well-rehearsed chant:

"There I was at twenty-six thousand. Four engines were out and the bomb bay was a ball of fire. I was in the waist wondering how to get the nose gunner's chute-pack to him. Fortunately, the flak was thick enough to walk on, so I stepped out of the window and ran up across the wing."

It had started as a raucous interruption, but now we were all smiling.

"You haven't heard about the camp's seventeenth general order? " one of them jested.

"What's the seventeenth general order?"

"No horror stories."

"No horror stories?"

"No. You see, we've all got a better one to tell than the one we're listening to, so we put together a sort of a composite for you new guys who want to hear one last horror story," one of them added.

"The real point is," another said, "we all know how to get in here; now we want to know how to get out."

Elimination of horror stories was a relief.

Our visitors left, with a last suggestion that we call a "room meeting" to decide how to handle the problems of living together in the restricted quarters.

We had a round of introductions. We accepted Porter's offer to be the official slicer of the daily issue of black bread for the room. We selected a chief cook to administer and supervise distribution of the food in our room's ration of twelve Red Cross parcels for the week. And we approved the resonant voice of a modest volunteer to be our reader.

After someone knocked on our door that evening, we huddled closely over the reader as he tested his hushed voice with, "Can you all hear this?" Clenched fists gripping imagined victory pumped silently but excitedly toward the ceiling as he read, "BBC reported today that significant advancements had been achieved by all forces of General Patton's Third Army along the entire. . . ."

If any space could have been considered "home" during our time at Stalag Luft I, it would have been the burlap pad we slept on with our joy box from Dulag at the head end. Every one of us would have said we all lived in exactly the same conditions; yet, after the war, there would be twenty-four different stories of what it was like.

At one of our room meetings, we questioned whether the abundance of time with little to do could cause us to become enemies of one another and forget that the Germans were our only real foe. Determined to maintain a sense of justice, we agreed that anyone would have a right to call a meeting. Any meeting dealing with room policy would be considered official; whoever called it would preside, and a decision would be based on a simple majority of the twenty-three votes of the others.

Acceptance of this attitude fostered a trust that precluded the need for meetings about many things; most could be handled with a loud and simple, "Does everybody agree?"

Many subjects of general interest became room-wide discussions with everyone participating or, at least, listening. One such session started with someone's suggestion that interest in our experience would be short-lived when we returned to the States. "Like the 'horror stories' here," he contended, "once they hear a few of these stories, they'll want whatever happened to you summarized in one sentence."

"How would you describe this room in one sentence?" a curious listener pondered aloud. A couple of vulgar responses were chuckled at but ignored because it sounded like a serious question. A long silence was finally broken with, "How about 'twenty-four men in a two-car garage'?"

"Make that a small two-car garage," another added, and many agreed that would be a good phrase to remember.

A narrow table with a long bench on each side seated twelve across the central third of the room. A window at one end of the table overlooked a large quadrangle surrounded by the other barracks of the compound. At the opposite end, the door opened to a common hall extending through the center of our barrack. Three long and deep bunk-shelves, occupying one wall from floor to ceiling, served the sleeping needs of eighteen prisoners. The other six were stacked three high across the room; food shelves and a small stove took the remaining corner.

A key to group harmony in our room was the system of dividing food to assure equal apportionment to everyone. When hearing of problems other rooms were having, someone from our room asserted proudly that our method was "accurate, not only to the crumb, but to the molecule."

The Red Cross parcel was a box approximately one foot square and five inches high. In addition to five packs of cigarettes, each parcel contained a packet of two dozen two-inch-square hard brown crackers; powdered milk adequate for a normal gallon, but more generally used as a mix for baking with crushed crackers; cheese or lunch meat; sugar cubes; sardines or a fruit jam or jelly; margarine; an occasional box of dried fruit, such as prunes; and a four-inch-long bar of hard chocolate called a "D-bar."

The Red Cross issued one parcel per week for every prisoner in Germany as each was reported captured throughout the war. Contents were intended only as a supplement to a basic German issue of bread, meat, and vegetables equal to quantities served to their own fighting troops, according to the Geneva Convention rules.

Delivery of the parcels to us by the Germans, however, decreased during the final months of the war. The Germans contended that increased American bombings destroyed transit routes and delayed delivery; we heard rumors about German civilians raiding trains to steal the food. According to later reports, the Germans had provided service that complied roughly with the Geneva agreement earlier in the war. However, as destruction of their country's systems forced them to spend more of their time on survival, they decreased service and rations to prisoners.

By the time we arrived in January of 1945, there was no meat or vegetable ration from the Germans, only bread, and Red Cross distributions had been cut to one-half: each room received twelve parcels. Within a few more weeks, the distribution was further cut to five parcels, then four, then two, and finally nothing by the middle of February.

We made the fortunate decision at one of our early room meetings to collectively shelve all food from the parcels as it was received. Our cook would then select items which were equally divided prior to serving. The equal portions were randomly distributed in a different order at every meal to further assure impartiality. When molecules could make a difference in an individual's survival capability, that kind of sharing is important.

Parcels were always similar, but often not identical. Occupants in rooms that tried to distribute contents directly to individuals always dealt with problems of comparative values, in addition to odd fractions, as quantities diminished later in the war.

The bread supply decreased only slightly as Germany tightened her belt. The daily ration allowed just over a one-inch-thick section from a four-inch-square loaf for each prisoner. Porter learned how to spend two hours each day evenly cutting eighth-inch-thick slices for everyone; it made us feel wealthier to know we'd had "four slices" of bread for lunch than to have the same weight in lesser numbers.

Because of our starvation diets, we considered the "black bread" quite tasty. But, because of its granular composition, we jested that it must be made from wood sawdust. We learned after the war that wood sawdust had indeed been used as a filler.

One person from each room went to the adjacent compound every morning to collect a pail full of coffee substitute, called "ersatz." It was a brew of roasted wood bark and yielded two cups of simulated coffee flavor for each prisoner.

When Red Cross parcels were no longer available, the Germans added a vegetable supplement in the form of a twelve-quart pail of "turnip soup" for each room. This provided prisoners one serving per day of one cup of unseasoned diced turnips plus a cup of the water they had been boiled in.

The time from the middle of February through March, when we subsisted on the meager rations of turnip soup and black bread, became known as the "starvation period." Medics estimated later that our intake then had diminished to approximately eight hundred calories per man per day. This increased the already serious weight loss, furthered physical weakening, and added new morale problems.

Weight loss had been a common experience for most prisoners during capture, transport, and temporary internments. However, those who had come to this Stalag earlier, when rations were still estimated to provide twelve to eighteen hundred calories, had been able to maintain or recover some of their strength; fate was less kind at this later time.

Although not always apparent, there existed the advantage of what today might be called group therapy. The "strong ones" appeared able to deal with emotional adversities without help from the others. But others benefited from recurring discussions of how we would survive.

The German word "kriegsgefangenen," describing us as war prisoners, was more than most of us preferred to pronounce. We commonly called ourselves "kriegies" because that part could have the upbeat interpretation of "warriors." Some of the syllables seemed more euphonious in repetition: if someone complained about our conditions too long or often, we used the chance to ridicule our enemy's language by reminding the complainer in a childish tone that he was "just being an ol' gefangen-angen-angen-angen."

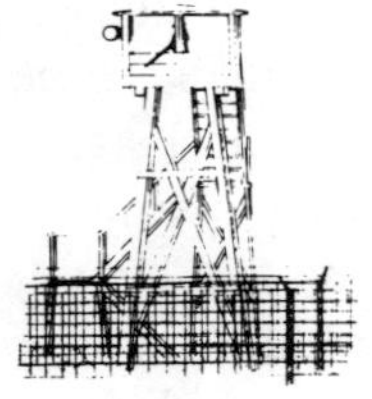

Chapter 11

Activities

Time slowed to a virtual stop. Days and nights were just like all the past days and nights and all possible future days and nights.

Some of the things we endured were despondency, fear, discouragement, suspicion, anxiety, resentment, doubt, boredom, guilt, skepticism, impatience, atrophy, sullenness, despair, antagonism, restlessness, anguish, depression, bewilderment, gloom, emaciation, disbelief, fatigue, hostility, desperation, irritability, monotony, weariness, debility, helplessness, deprivation, weakness, disappointment, starvation, animosity, regret, faintness, uncertainty, alienation, and pessimism.

I've listed the items above so the impact of the story isn't weakened when these are omitted from the remaining narrative. The total absence of negative aspects from movies and television shows about prison life infuriated most former prisoners of war in the months and years after their return. Incarceration wasn't just one long series of laughs at German stupidity, as depicted in many of those shows. But there was often humor, because prisoners deliberately produced it to offset effects of the negative emotions listed above.

We facetiously called our camp "Beautiful Barth on the Baltic." We couldn't see water from our compound, but we knew we were at the base of a peninsula, with distances to the sea varying from less than a mile to several miles, depending on the direction.

If given the chance, almost every prisoner would have left at a moment's notice without a thought of glancing back at his joy box. The word "almost" qualifies that statement, because, when liberation finally came, two Britons who had been imprisoned for the five years since Dunkerque were reportedly hesitant about leaving; they had become apprehensive of the uncertainties of freedom.

Two high barbed wire fences surrounded our compound with loose loops of more barbed wire randomly coiled in the space between them. One additional strand of wire, stretching between short stakes ten feet inside the fence and a foot above the ground, was called a "warning wire." This was as close to the fence as we were allowed; beyond that strand, the guards watching from the towers would shoot. We were told they had proved that in the past.

Just inside the warning wire was a wide and worn path. It was rough and icy in the winter, muddy in the early spring, and dusty when it dried. Walking was one of the common ways for prisoners to pass time, and it was also considered by most as a way to retain strength. Prisoners preferred "the perimeter" because the snow beyond the wire was white and clean in the winter, grass was green in the spring, and the weeds in the fields were real and healthy.

From soon after dawn, when the Germans removed the bars from barracks doors, to just before dark, when they replaced the bars, except for roll calls, walkers paced the perimeter, generally in pairs or as singles. It was a good way to get to know the feelings of a roommate, but there was seldom any effort to mingle with those from other rooms or barracks.

A common fence on one border was shared with North Compound Two. Although the gates between compounds were always locked except to those with special permission from the Germans, it was possible to talk through the fence to the walkers in the next compound and, with cooperation of neighbor prisoners, to relay messages to others beyond. This is how Hartfield and I learned that all six crew members taken with us were in other parts of Stalag Luft I.

The distance around our perimeter was roughly one-quarter of a mile. I took that walk an average of six times a day for a total of two hundred miles while waiting for liberation. That number appeared typical for most prisoners, and the debate continued over whether less walking to conserve calories or more to get the exercise was better.

Although the five-minute circuit of the perimeter provided a break from the room's boredom, totals of each day's walks took only half an hour. There had to be other activities to accompany the endless conversations. And there were; we were surprised at how the collective ingenuity provided them.

An initial key to generating such pastimes was the awareness that nothing should be disposed of without considering possible uses for it. That attitude happily brought a recycling of almost everything that came into the room. The sequence of uses resulted in no apparent waste. Paper labels, carefully peeled from cans of food in the Red Cross parcels, were tucked behind slivers or into cracks to serve as colorful decorations over the drab walls. When one of these was replaced later by a new choice, the back of the paper was used as a temporary diary or to develop a poetic capability inspired by someone's thoughts for a poem. An artistically folded creation generally preceded the paper's final use as a fire starter.

Kitchen knives were converted to small handsaws as needed by abrading a series of notches into their edges on the corners of the bricks our stove was mounted on. Special skive tools were similarly made for whittling. Wood stock was judiciously sawed from unneeded sections of footboards on the bunk shelves.

The soldered seams were cut from all metal food containers and the metal sheets were flattened into sections for assembly into baking pans of all shapes and sizes. With a strand of yarn pressed inside the Z-type seams, there was rarely a water leak that couldn't be sealed with a few deft taps in the right places by the metal crafters.

While a hot fire was in progress to warm the room, the soldered seam strips that had been removed from cans earlier were heated in the coal briquettes to reclaim the solder. The molten solder was poured into moulds made by whittlers, and the resulting "POW, Clipped Wings," with a silhouette similar to those formerly awarded for completing Service Schools, could be "sold" for cigarettes to the right buyer at the right price as a novel chest decoration.

The playing cards in the deck issued to our room by the American welcome committee were so wilted from use that they drooped over a finger like old paper currency, but as paper became available, we cut and marked small rectangles for several decks: "JD" in the corners meant the card was the jack of diamonds. Group games were never played in our room, but there were almost always a couple of games of solitaire in progress on the bunks or table.

Any knowledge seemed always to be happily shared. I learned how to play over twenty different games of solitaire.

Hoping I was starting a personal project that might outlast the war, I took one of the large handkerchiefs from my joy box and sketched detailed figures on it to be embroidered later with thread from the sewing kit. After lightly outlining and making many corrections, I completed scenes depicting a pair of large feathered wings across the top half joined by a center circle containing the letters "POW." A shield in the lower quadrant listed crew members' names, and a B-24 dropping bombs bearing the letters of our target occupied the remaining corner.

The embroidery was completed after a few weeks, but the war seemed to have progressed very little. The finished handiwork appeared dull, partly because the only two colors of thread in the military sewing kit were sun tan and olive drab. I noticed that both pairs of socks from the joy box were a flecked tan color with a wide band of white ribbing at the top; trimming above the ribbing consisted of red and blue yarn which could be unraveled without damaging the socks.

The second handkerchief with the four colors and improved handicraft produced a much more pleasing finished product — but war progress still hadn't seemed to have changed significantly.

Considerable effort was sometimes spent in attempts to present new kinds of humor. A little sign resembling one that might have been planted by a professional landscaper once appeared beside a barrack along the beaten perimeter path, bearing the message, "Please Stay Off Our Mud."

Numerous hopefuls aspired to immortalize past heroics in living poetry. Many of these found that merely placing, at the end of phrases, their selections of glaring sun, bomb run, no fun and overheated gun

. . . did not, as they'd hoped t'would,
Yield poem-reading fun.

Even worse,
As aloud for critique they'd rehearse,
They'd learn lack of meter made their verse,
For lauding heroics, adverse.

Time spent on such endeavors was always well used, however; it displaced ugly feelings toward incarceration with awareness that better things were out there if we could endure the wait.

Some authors used lengthy titles to indicate intended meanings of their poetic efforts. After rumors that we might be repatriated in a trade for German soldiers captured in the Battle of the Bulge, I attempted a terse summary of timely feelings with a jest at grandiose titles as follows:

Repatriation Contemplation

I'll burn my board and blanket,
I'll break my bowl and spoon,
And the day I think of this place again,
Will be a day too soon.

"No, the tip goes through this loop first and then over . . . ," could be heard outside from burly kriegies teaching basic rules of knitting to clumsy students on the sunny side of the barracks when the weather warmed in March. Sweaters with huge holes in the elbows had been unraveled for yarn stock to replace socks with huge holes in the heels and toes. Shared toothbrushes with handles abraded to fine needle tips would produce a rhythmic clicking a few days later as the happy knitter anticipated the cozy warmth his new skill would provide.

Generally, whenever we were able to keep our spirits up, we could find ways to pass the time. But we were annoyed after hearing that our captors had taken credit for our ingenuity in a report to the International Red Cross stating that their prisoners were kept happy with games provided by German camp administrators.

A significant factor in keeping group morale above the survival level was the ability to discuss pros and cons of everything that did, would, or could affect our existence. Because we couldn't improve conditions, outliving them was our chief goal; this made progress of the war a primary concern. We essentially trusted everything reported nightly on the single-sheet news abridgement, the POW WOW. Discussions regarding that news therefore went directly into the postoperative analysis of why other strategy hadn't been used which could have resulted in more success sooner.

We occasionally jested that the hindsight of any one of us was far better than the foresight of all of Eisenhower's highly paid staff.

General Patton was our favorite. When his divisions moved, the action seemed always to be clever and dramatic. If the POW WOW reported that progress was slow in some area because of problems with supplies, a typical comment was, "Why didn't they give Patton that job? He could have taken the whole army fifty miles on a gallon of gas."

After Allied forces had fully recovered from the confusion of the Battle of the Bulge, we started discussing ways to vault what was assumed to be the European war's final hurdle, the Rhine. Many agreed Germany would capitulate shortly after that crossing was accomplished. Conversations overheard on perimeter walks confirmed that hope for early success in that area was widespread.

Allowing a logical number of weeks, someone posted a sign in our hall with the morale-boosting slogan, "Across the Rhine before March 9." When progress slowed, another changed the sign to, "Across the Rhine by April 9." After worse news a few days later, a pessimist added four years with the modified, "Across the Rhine by '49," and, as progress stalled, someone temporarily concluded that rally of hope with, "Across the Rhine by '99."

Our elation peaked on 7 March when a *faux pas* on the part of the German demolition corps left the Ludendorff Bridge standing at Remagen and opportunistic Allied troops dashed across. Despondency returned, however, as fierce German resistance slowed hopes for an instant sweep into Berlin.

At times when there seemed to be little or nothing to hope for, we tried to find ways to laugh at our plight. One day, someone adjusted the words of the patriotic march "Over There" and suggested the room try it in chorus. With a capable leader, we lustily sang:

Over here, over here,
We are over, we're staying over,
And we won't go back,
'Till it's over over here.

The original version was only promises, but we could now laugh at the ludicrous truth of our rendition.

Much of the room's conversation evolved from wishful thinking about possible liberation that might occur before the war ended. A sequence typically started with the justification, "Listen, eight thousand troops who would sooner fight than wait are worth retrieving." The argument then followed that our peninsula had no military defenses and could be easily invaded from the Baltic. Excitement would increase, until a dismal reminder from another bunk area advised, "Before you guys start figuring how many of what kind of boats you'll need, remember: very few people know we're here, and the ones who do don't give a damn."

Rumors about various subjects were continually overheard and brought back to the room for review of plausibility.

Fortunately, there were some kriegies who always tried to keep humor alive. One of these provided a fresh approach to conversational time-passing, making use of the general assumption that higher military ranks are privy to highly classified information: he typically prefaced revelation of pretended news with, "I was walking the perimeter behind Gabreski, and he was quietly telling his adjutant about the Allies' latest plan to. . . ." A surprise air-drop of troops on our peninsula to capture Berlin from the north, while German defenses were days away at the battlefronts, could then become an enjoyable way to imagine that the war would soon be over.

Forms were available on which to write the allowed two letters and four postal cards each month. It reportedly took four to six months to get an answer. Few were sent out from our compound because we expected the war to end before that. Also, it was felt that anything other than, "I'm fine. We're being treated well," wouldn't be mailed by the Germans. No personal mail was ever received in our room.

The response to one prisoner's good manners was unfortunately sensational enough to be circulated through the fence from another compound. He had found the knitter's name and address tucked inside the sweater in his joy box at Dulag Luft, and he had used one of his cards to thank her as a needy prisoner of war. Her answer indicated disgust because she had hoped her efforts would go "to someone who had the guts to get out and fight for his country."

"What the hell makes that broad think —," someone started to ask.

"Nothing makes that broad think," another interrupted during the pause.

But, despite pseudomacho retorts, the scorn had cut deeply into fragile morale, even deeper than some of the news about resumption of labor strikes for higher wages back home "because the war was nearly over."

Discussions about all kinds of food and all phases of its existence from source to consumption shared time with talks of survival and the war's progress. Kriegies with cooking capabilities reviewed ingredients of recipes for favorite dishes. Being from a rural part of one of the northern states, I had never heard of pecan pie, but it sounded like it was well worth living for. Most of us agreed to send recipes for various things to each other after the war. We promised ourselves to never again inhale the exhilarating aromas from a candy store or bakery shop without stopping to purchase "at least a little something."

Our intentions seemed so very sincere at that time; months later, however, after returning to a land flowing with milk and honey and pecan pies and candies and bakeries, many of us were reminded of the negative aspects of overindulgence.

We were surprised at one time to realize that some subjects were never talked about. Shortly after everyone awakened on a morning late in the starvation period, one of our better comedians started the day with, "You know what, fellas?" We listened, because unique commentary often followed that opening. "I had a wet dream last night," he added. After a shocked silence, we enjoyed a rare unison roar of laughter; we had not only lost that capability, we had totally forgotten the term and its meaning.

Some tried to continue the humor with, "Did you think you were having an affair with Axis Sally?" But we soon got serious, wondering how previously prime subjects like women and sex could slip totally out of the consciousness of virile young twenty-year-olds.

We eventually agreed that we were no longer virile. That had originally been considered a completely pessimistic view. The few "older" married men in their later twenties then informed us that they thought of their wives often, but only as images which they hoped would take on life again when they returned. We concluded that nature was protecting us from ourselves by removing other concerns so we could concentrate on survival. To restore hope, so we could change the subject, we then decided a few ham-and-eggs breakfasts would restore what we hadn't realized we were missing.

On one occasion, we learned about the camp's history from a resident of one of the first compounds. He had been admitted to our area as a volunteer on a camp duty routine and was directed to our room by another kriegie to meet an acquaintance from his home town. He stayed for a couple of hours to answer questions about his previous two years in our camp.

He remembered when the men enjoyed reminiscing about their women, but that was when the Germans were still providing a meat, bread, and vegetables diet and the Red Cross food supplement was a full parcel per week. In those days, group showers had been provided frequently, gates between the compounds were always left open, and all Germans were still sure that they would win the war.

The man remembered that many tunnels were dug below floor boards removed for that purpose; the dirt was hidden under other flooring. There had been numerous escapes, with prisoners being recaptured on the peninsula. A rumor persisted that one escapee had made it back to England, but no one knew if it was true or if the rumor recirculated for the sake of keeping hope alive.

We enjoyed the visitor's enthusiasm during a story about reversing the odds on one of the guard dogs. Everyone hated the dogs, including animal lovers with similar pets back home. They were huge German Shepherds trained for vicious attacks on throats or genitals of kriegsgefangenen. In addition to the two numerical roll calls in the quadrangle each day, there were occasional "kriegie roll calls" in the rooms. Dogs were released in the hall to prevent room-switching, guards called occupants' names, and kriegies answered with their prison ID numbers.

Our informant explained their careful plans for a day when there was only one dog in the hall. After their room had been checked and the guards were in another room at the opposite end of the building, they opened their door against a bench placed to admit the dog's skull but not his shoulders. Six hands held the door when the victim charged into their trap, and a blur of kicking boots bloodied the dog's head just short of unconsciousness before he could yelp to alert the guards. The Germans rechecked all rooms, but nobody could figure out how a dog could be decommissioned in those few minutes. The prisoners, who suffered bruised ankles, had felt it was well worth it. There was always more than one dog in the hall at all subsequent roll calls.

When the visitor left, we knew we had derived a vicarious satisfaction from that final story. Someone thinking aloud probably summarized our feelings with, "You know, it's odd; we often feel that we sort of lost our part of the war. It's a good feeling to think that some of our kind won at least one of the battles."

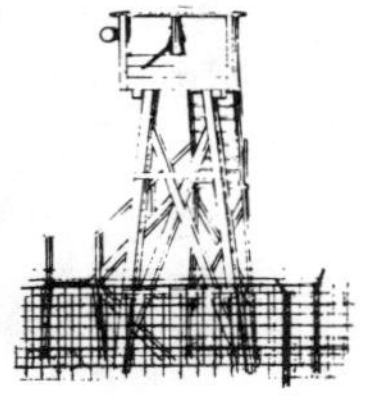

Chapter 12

The Russians Are Coming

In the first weeks after our arrival, there were attempts to initiate "educational" opportunities like those more common in older compounds. A room reserved for that purpose in another barrack was called "the Library." Chaplains also used the room with their clients when they visited the compound. There were a few dozen books that had been donated by the YMCA, and there were a few volunteers who shared knowledge as teachers without the help of teaching aids or "learning supplies."

Because of the uncertain future, however, motivation faltered in subjects unrelated to our wait for freedom, and such rooms were converted to living quarters as prisoners continued arriving in increasing numbers.

Things we learned from unique behavior or spontaneous reaction to the fear and boredom of incarceration would instead be the lessons we remembered.

During the middle of one night, I awoke with a not uncommon severe backache, sore shoulder, and the usual need to make the short trip down the hall to our "night-latrine." After sliding from the top shelf quietly to avoid waking others, I took the three steps to the door and was startled by movement of a large dark blob behind our little shelf. It became motionless instantly as I stopped to focus my sight. My senses unmistakably identified the crouched figure of a roommate with one hand in a bowl of chocolate fudge. We had grated the chocolate and mixed it with powdered milk and water earlier that night in preparation for a meager treat later in the week.

Bewildered, I turned and continued through the door, and when I returned minutes later, the roommate was in bed. Conflicting feelings of anger and sympathy prevented sleep for the next hour.

Just before lunch the next day, our cook called what he insisted was the most important room meeting we'd ever had. There was attentive interest as he obviously suppressed his emotions while opening with a slow and deliberate, "We have among us — right here in this very room —," and his voice quavered angrily as he lifted the bowl, tipped it forward, and snarled, "a son of a bitch whose fingers have left this type of gouges in our chocolate fudge."

The guilty kriegie's line of sight flicked in and out of line with mine in the scary quiet. When the speaker suggested that someone among "the twenty-three others who toss and turn all night" must have seen him, I could foresee nothing but more trouble for everyone if the thief were exposed.

After another long silence, our cook concluded, "If that's the way you bastards want to be, the meeting's over." The incident was never again discussed, but our cook said later he had "lost heart" and that we should elect someone else to oversee food concerns.

What we called the "night-latrine" was a little room at the end of the hall with a wooden box on the floor, which the two hundred of us used after the doors were barred at dusk. Liquids ran through the bottom of the box and between the floor boards to the ground below. In the morning, the box was carried to the day-latrine in the corner of the compound and emptied.

I was told by a medic in the States many months later that I had probably had a urinary tract infection when I described the numerous seemingly useless trips to that little room during many nights. Determined to remember the total, I kept an accurate count through the seventh trip one night, and then lost track in an exhausted stupor.

I was in one such stupor on returning from the night-latrine when I became curious about a recurring noise in the moonlight outside the barrack. The glass in one section of the window in our door had been broken for some time, and I knew I could get my head through if I carefully avoided the jagged pieces around the edges. After I had my head through, I turned it and saw a guard dog scratching at the base of a barrack support-post ten feet away.

Shocked into alert consciousness, I pulled back and bumped my head against the top of the frame. The dog's leap overshadowed the entire window as he emitted terrifying combinations of roars and growls, but I was already several feet away from the door. The blinding beam from a searchlight in the nearest guard tower came on while I hurried back into the room and under my blanket. Another light beamed in from across the compound, then another, a few doors opened in our hall, and a couple of roommates mumbled sleepy questions about what might be happening.

When people discussed the noise and lights the next morning and wondered if there had been an escape attempt, I was too embarrassed to explain. Red fingertips after checking the scratch on my scalp indicated I had lost a few drops of blood. But I didn't want to hear jokes about possibly getting a Purple

Heart for that wound, or about the dog being smarter than I; so I remained quiet — and glad that I hadn't lost my head.

After the weather warmed up one morning in early March, the German guard force confirmed things we had heard about their dogs' capabilities with a demonstration in the field just outside our compound. They probably called it a training session, but since it had been done in front of other compounds in previous years we felt the word "demonstration" defined their real purpose.

Twenty dogs were paraded past our fence by their trainers, who carried equipment. The trainers set up racks and attached simulated torsos made from bundles of straw wrapped in burlap. The dogs then charged their targets from various distances on command to tear a piece from the top or bottom of the dummy in accord with their training. After the snarling leap, they coughed out straw and shook shredded burlap from their jowls while returning to approving trainers.

We continued our perimeter walks during the long hour and tried to pretend we hardly noticed, but the Germans knew they had impressed us.

The starvation process had actually begun for most of us when we were first shot down or captured, but with prime health and youth the only effect during the first weeks seemed to be hunger. Gauntness and weakness became more evident with the severe malnutrition that followed the reduction of the food parcels. Porter slid along the bunks to the floor immediately after waking and standing up one morning. As we crowded around him, he responded to our, "Hey, you okay?" with a confused smile and, "Of course, I'm okay," as he struggled to his knees. "I guess I tried to get up too fast," he added. "It seemed to be sort of a blackout."

We soon heard about similar occurrences from other rooms. A few days later, it happened to someone else in our room, and after a few more days I responded to that question, myself, while pushing up from the floor, grinning: "Ya, I'm all right. I guess I forgot to hold the wall." I then understood the reason for the term "blackout." I remembered a brief darkening that seemed to turn vision black before the momentary unconsciousness.

It happened to others in the following weeks, and we learned to remind each other not to change position, especially from reclining to standing, too suddenly. The experience was slightly different from fainting, and our word for it was more acceptable to us; "fainting" connoted a weakness, but a blackout was something "dumb" we had allowed because we had moved too quickly without thinking.

Two Germans entered one morning, calling out the name of one of our roommates. "Vould you come mit unce, bitta?" That was German for "please" — they were being too polite. After turning pale, he walked out with them. We turned our shocked looks toward his crew mate on the next bunk, who finally stammered, "I — I'm — I'm sure — I'm quite sure I know what it's about, but I can't say anything."

We waited in a stunned silence for ten minutes, until our door reopened and the roommate hurried to his bunk, saying, "I got to go. They're waiting for me in the hall."

He rolled his pad and blanket and tucked them under an arm with his joy box. He and his crew mate each clamped a hand on the other's shoulder and stared into each other's eyes for several seconds. He turned at the door to say, "I, ah, I don't know anything. I had a "P" on my dog tags, but they didn't trust it. They've been checking ever since and they just showed me my family tree from way back. I'm Jewish." He then forced his lips into a smile and raised a hand for a hesitant wave.

There was silence again. Then the crew mate said, "That was it." We inquired through the fence later to learn that he had been taken to a special barrack in another compound where the Germans kept other Americans like him segregated.

I decided to take a fast perimeter walk at dusk one evening just before lock-in. Near the halfway point as I approached the compound's gate, I could see the guard crew coming in to bar the doors. Everyone else was inside. I knew the dogs would be released soon, so I turned onto a diagonal course directly toward my barrack. I stooped to pick up a small brown object along the path and slipped it into my pocket without breaking the rhythm of my pace — I knew it was a potato the size of a golf ball.

I successfully disguised my excitement until bedtime, despite subconscious thoughts that were planning a cermonious night. In the total quiet after everyone was in bed, I first pondered all possibilities of how the potato could have gotten there. I deduced that one of the few volunteers who worked in the German supplies area had stolen it, that he must have had his pocket filled for one to have fallen out, that he was from my barrack or the adjacent one because he had used that path, and that he had returned from work just prior to my walk, or the potato would have been found by someone else previously.

I thanked God for taking care of us all and for the presence of this unique occurrence, and I next considered whether I should present my find to the room. Since we were in the starvation period, the only way it could be shared would be to shred it into the turnip soup. However, this potato had never been intended for the group; it was different from the half-canteen-cup of barley soup near Nuremberg, and the chocolate fudge a few weeks earlier. So, after rubbing off the dried mud, I ate the potato and concluded my silent ritual.

After dismissal from the morning roll call in the quadrangle, we occasionally returned to the barracks to find the doors locked until German guards had completed a search for the source of our newspaper, for indications of escape intentions, and so on. When we were readmitted to the barracks on one such morning, we found everything from our joy boxes strewn around in disarray. The tiny red cloth that had held the needles in our sewing kits had been torn out. We learned later that a prisoner had just used a few of these to fashion insignia simulating that of the Red Cross medics in a nearly successful disguise to escape through the main gate.

We returned from a long wait through several rechecks of the roll call on a bitterly cold and windy morning to find a military carpenter completing repairs to our barrack door. He scowled as the two hundred of us crowded shivering to within six feet of him to wait for reentry to the warmth of the barrack. He remained kneeling beside the door long after his work was finished, and a kriegie finally asked if we could enter. There was no answer, but the carpenter watched intently as the kriegie's hand moved tentatively toward the door.

Suddenly the German's hammer struck like a cobra; blood flowed onto the kriegie's hand instantly and the crowd surged forward during one step of rage. We all checked our action simultaneously after the step because we knew that further reaction would merely bring machine gun bullets rattling into our group from the guard towers.

After another long wait, the warmly dressed German sauntered away. We hurried into the hall to cluster around the injured prisoner, but he reassured us that there were only surface bruises to the back of his hand.

Retributive emotions then began venting as we started the return to our rooms. Someone called down the hall loudly, "Did everyone get a good look at that son of a bitch?"

"Yup."

"Yeah."

"Remember fellas, in another month or couple when we get out of here, we got a job to do. We gotta fix that Kraut's door before we go home. Okay?"

"Ya."

"Okay."

"Everybody brings a hammer. Okay?"

"Yep."

"Okay."

"We won't need any nails because, countin' toes and fingers, he should have twenty of his own we can start with."

"We can find a lot more than that. Those bastards all look alike to me now."

Our morale was buoyed a bit on a later date while watching a play presented by a group formed in the earlier days of the camp's existence. The play spoofed our plight and suggested ridiculously humorous ways by which we could traverse the Baltic Sea to freedom in Sweden. It was delightful to hear ourselves laugh, but jesting at our own misfortunes never maintained good spirits very long.

We wished the war's progress would become consistent so we could trust our hopes for freedom by some predictable time. But we never thought of looking toward the eastern front for liberation. Before those of us in the room had been shot down, the Russians were carrying out a valiant counteroffensive, driving Germans out of their country toward the west. But the last we had heard from our POW WOW back in January was that they had been stopped along the Vistula River around Warsaw, over three hundred miles east of Berlin.

"Our boys" had recovered from the Battle of the Bulge and started drives which later bogged down. They crossed the Rhine and bogged down again. We didn't know about the politics of war; we didn't understand about special meetings between Churchill and Roosevelt and Stalin on special islands and at special resorts. So, every check was hard to believe and adjust to, and our thoughts always turned inward toward self-pity.

One of the rooms down the hall kept a "morale chart." They posted an average from one through ten on the wall each day after a room survey. When they became experienced at keeping the records, they felt that the chart helped to improve their outlook during a rising trend, but had a negative effect while feelings worsened.

Our spirits improved briefly on a warm day in March when we were taken to another compound for our first shower. Undressing for the group shower at first indicated that the good times had returned. But then we looked up to notice that the recent months had turned young masculine physiques into hollow, bony bodies. We didn't talk. Finishing the shower was a dutiful activity, not a pleasure. Feelings included embarrassment and shame. Because of the changing course of events, this was also the last shower provided by the Germans.

I walked the perimeter alone to try to reorient my attitude. Several months earlier, we were everything that our country had asked for. I remembered packing into a large recreation hall with squadron members at Yuma, Arizona, to attend a radio broadcast about our activities; that was what the station's listeners wanted to hear about at that time. A very adept master of ceremonies said we were today's and tomorrow's heroes, while we faked modest disclaiming murmurs.

He explained before airtime what his hand signals would mean and what the audience prompters would do. His wide palm had quieted the room, his index finger followed the sweep hand on the wall clock to the last second when he tipped the microphone to say, "The Yuma Army Air Base presents": cymbals crashed, a large curtain behind him flew open to expose a huge military band that blared our song, and there was thunderous applause as he shouted, "Gunners with Wings!" into the mike.

Now we were skeletons with skin: this was the tomorrow he had referred to, and nobody cared. We had accomplished nothing, except to get ourselves shot down and captured.

I reentered the room to hear a typical discussion about how long we could last on the current number of calories. Someone repeated the argument, "You've got it good here. If the Japs had gotten you, they'd be workin' ya to death on fish heads and rice three times a week." One of the emotional stalwarts quipped, "Look, when you guys lie down to die, I'm gonna boil my shoes to make soup."

I did something I had seen a few others doing, probably as an aftereffect of noticing the changes in our bodies during the shower. I pushed my sleeve above my elbow and studied the motions of muscles and tendons in my forearm as I moved different fingers. There seemed to be something indecent about watching body parts that I had never seen before, so I pulled the sleeve down and buttoned it.

We were curious one morning when we learned that our compound commander, Colonel Gabreski, was calling a group meeting. It surprised us at first when he expressed concern over the deteriorating morale, and when he repeated the trite warning about losing our part of the war by succumbing to negative feelings. He welcomed anyone to audit his lifestyle and disprove rumors about larger rations for him due to rank, but he added that they must bring their own food because he had none to share.

After reviewing his comments later, we agreed he had quite eloquently rephrased a well-known theme in a well-meant effort to lead a change in attitude. We appreciated his attempt.

The POW WOW reported that Russian forces had been reclaiming territory from the Germans in a frenetic drive toward Berlin since crossing the Vistula. We were passively pleased about that; it seemed they were putting the "lend-lease" equipment our country had given them to good use. But they were too far away to make any difference in our future.

Apparently the German Military saw that unchecked advance as a dangerous trend and wished we were their ally instead of their enemy so we could help them: a few weeks later signs appeared in our compound offering release from prisoner status to all who would fight on their eastern front "to help save the world from Bolshevism."

Whenever the Germans had questioned our sanity in previous months, their remark had been, "Bis du frick?" Now we turned their question; we were astonished — the Russians were our allies!

The first signs of German change in attitude had not been that obvious. They had a supply of lard to give us: they apologetically explained to our leaders that they could do nothing about getting Red Cross parcels to the Stalag, and they did not have adequate food supplies to increase the rations they provided; but they had lard to share. This was new: they had never cared about us at all before. A few pounds of lard was delivered to each room. It didn't look or smell edible, so we stored it.

News from the POW WOW reported again that action continued to be only moderate along the western front, while the Russian drive from the Vistula toward the Oder remained relentless.

Our interest in the Russians increased. Several of them were periodically brought in with a wagon to clean the day-latrine used by the two thousand men in our compound. (The word "clean" was a misnomer; the place was always as filthy after they left as before. The purpose of their service was simply to make it possible to continue use of the facility.)

We had always heard that the Germans treated Russians incomprehensibly worse than they did Americans. I had heard more recently that some of our kriegies slipped cigarettes to Russian workers when guards weren't watching.

On my next trip to the latrine while the cleaning crew was there, I held a cigarette up toward a busily working, burly Russian with a bushy crop of dirty hair jutting out from below his cap. I was surprised when he ignored me and stepped outside. He apparently hadn't trusted my check for German guards: when he stepped back in, his motions were so fast I followed them only in retrospect. The cigarette vanished from my hand, his index finger shot into his bushy hair, the cigarette disappeared into the little tunnel his finger had made, and he continued working and ignoring me.

I first felt he was crude, but he flashed a split-second smile and snapped a short nod as he went outside again and I knew he was concerned for his well-being in case our exchange was noticed.

Another report in the POW WOW said Russian forces were nearing the Oder River. Then, one night, our light went out — electrical power was out everywhere. The Germans told us to blame the Russians; our power came from the Stettin area, ninety miles to the southeast, and the source had been damaged. Our emotions were confused, but only briefly. It sounded like good news. If Uncle Sam couldn't get to us, we'd be happy to be liberated by Uncle Joe Stalin!

The light had been very dim, but it was adequate for hobbies and solitaire until bedtime. The country boys among us remembered childhood days of kerosene lamps and lanterns. The lard we hadn't eaten would burn if we only had a wick to make a lamp. As we tried to explain wicks to the city boys, we realized they were just like the web belts we were wearing.

The belts, which had been trimmed to a one-half-inch length beyond the buckle, according to military regulations, when we had first become prisoners, now dangled loosely. Someone sawed the spare five inches from his belt to try a test burn. A sardine can with the cover slotted and bent to support the wick, produced a lamp. After melting a bit of lard, and with a little priming, we had a light nearly as good as the one before the power outage.

Each of us contributed the excess lengths from our belts for future wick stock. One who had been "chubby" when he was captured tossed in a six-inch length; a couple who had been thin had only four inches to give; but typical spare lengths were five inches. That reduction from what had been militarily trim and healthy waists, seemed scary at first. The reaction was easily put aside, however, with the reminder that this had all been discovered because of good signs of progress on the eastern front.

An excitingly new kind of message then flashed around the compound, one morning, that far better signs were now evident. When it was quiet at night, if the wind was right, and if the clouds were right, and if the moon was right, and if one was patient, Russian artillery could be heard!

We stood motionless that night in the hall near the door and held our breath. When someone's finger went up, we strained and faintly heard, "Boom . . . Boom, Boom, Boom . . . Boom . . . Boom, Boom . . . Boom." Fists of victory pumped gleefully toward the ceiling again: these were the most thrilling sounds we had heard since capture.

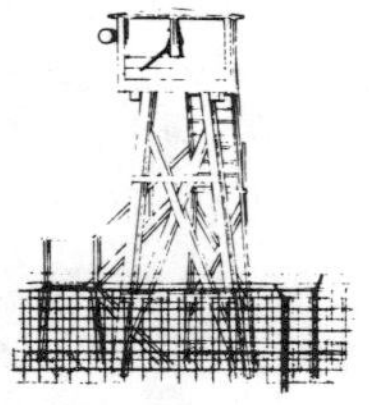

Chapter 13

The Germans Are Gone!

We were not surprised when the Russian forces bogged down on the banks of the Oder River before crossing on their drive toward the west. We had learned to accept a common fact about ground warfare: supplies and equipment that have lagged behind must be brought up before an assault on the next major barrier. They had traversed 250 miles since Warsaw and the Vistula. The German defense was fierce now, because another breakthrough would bring the Russian wrath the last fifty miles to the ultimate battle of Berlin.

We knew it would be a matter of several weeks. The actual number wasn't important because we didn't have to wonder if our hopes of progress were merely wishful thinking: we could stand in the hall on a quiet night and hear the guns. Our morale continued to improve. Speculation about imagined rescue or possible ways to escape could now be replaced with more realistic wonder about how the war would end. Might every German have to be killed or forcibly disarmed? That was what the order from Hitler had seemed to imply, and the Germans whom we could see didn't appear to know how to stop the war.

Research in radar and experimental work to improve its application to warfare were apparently continuing in a building just outside our camp near the older compounds. A small German plane, piloted by someone who had been jestingly dubbed "Fearless Fosdick," still occasionally circled over the building to drop tinsel. When strands of the tinsel drifted on breezes into our compound, we were reminded of days when we dropped it to confuse German radar on bomb runs.

The Germans needed space to house the men they were shooting down with existing weapons more than they needed to improve their weapons. As their artillery was pushed back into ever smaller areas, new prisoner entries averaged one thousand per month for our camp alone. There were rumors in late March that our total was nearing ten thousand kriegies.

These new prisoners in the spring were hungry but healthy. Athletic equipment that had come from the YMCA to older compounds earlier was brought out for softball games in our quadrangle. We watched new robust Americans with some curiosity; because they hadn't shared our recent past, they seemed like a different people.

Behavior of the Germans continued to become more unpredictable. A prisoner in another compound was reported shot by a guard because of new orders in March to "shoot to kill" any prisoner if there was any attempt to escape or any doubt of intent to conform with German regulations. The orders were supposedly from the military hierarchy, initially from Hitler.

When we opened our door in response to a knock one morning, however, two elderly German guards spread broad smiles across their faces and said, "Vee come yust to wisit," as they sauntered into the room. We didn't want to visit with them, and they didn't know how to start their "wisit." After several tense minutes, our hobbies and solitaire games quietly resumed; the wisitors nodded smiles in all directions, said, "Haf a gooten day. Gooten-bye," and left to make similar goodwill calls in other rooms.

We had obeyed orders to stay inside when formations of bombers were sighted entering our area in early April, but we crowded toward windows in the exit doors in the hall when the planes were jubilantly identified as "ours." We took turns glimpsing the most thrilling sight in months, until the guard in the nearest tower suddenly whipped the muzzle of his machine gun toward us. No shots were fired, but we scampered and tumbled back into the hall because we didn't know if this guard, too, might "doubt our intent to conform."

A rumor that a small shipment of Red Cross parcels had been received in the camp was hard to believe after the seven-week starvation period, but each room did receive a couple of parcels. We forgot the war's progress for several hours while cautioning ourselves to conserve wisely and planning preparations for meager "goodies." It seemed that those Germans who had let their own people pilfer boxes en route to us earlier now wanted our ultimate sympathy more than our current ration of food.

The heaviest smokers among us seemed to be as elated about the return of cigarette rations as they were with the extra food. Some insured their habit's future through written agreements with those who had reverted to a nonsmoking status. They exchanged home addresses and gleefully signed promissory notes for $10.00 per pack payable upon return home. Someone wondered if the debtors would be as happy to sign the checks in the future as they had been to sign the notes, and others wondered if the creditors would ever care, once they returned home.

We had been intrigued initially by the apparent accuracy and minute detail of a large hand-drawn map of Germany that appeared in the hall of our barrack. One man of every ten-man bomber crew was a navigator, and it became obvious that the nine hundred navigators interned here had all studied their maps well as they had collectively criss-crossed almost every square mile of this country. We were grateful to those who had passed their time providing reference maps for all barracks, but we wondered what the guards' reactions would be when they saw pins in the map supporting strands of yarn designating encroaching battle fronts.

The total lack of response shown by the guards spoke to us as convincingly as any verbal communication could have. They knew they would soon lose the war; they only wished they could lose it exclusively to us, because it would be far easier to elicit sympathy from Americans, ninety-five percent of whom were comfortably isolated in a homeland thousands of miles away, than from Russians, whose homeland they had recently trampled and desecrated.

An unexpected announcement informed us that more food parcels had arrived. The new total didn't bring deliveries up to the quota shipped from the States, but it was far better than we had had in many weeks and it confirmed our observation that German guards had changed their attitudes toward us. Then a large bulletin board appeared at the edge of our quadrangle near the compound's gate, and each day the Germans posted a summary of news of the European war. It was interesting to note that the essence of their news now compared quite well with ours from the POW WOW.

It confused us somewhat, however, to read phrases like "enduring efforts of valiant Germans to save the world from the horrors of Bolshevism," and the "relentless drives of never-ending hordes" of the "barbarians from the east." Many of their adjectives and adverbs sounded interestingly similar to those we had read in our newspapers in the first weeks of our war with the Japanese two years earlier.

At a roll call assembly in the quadrangle on the thirteenth of April, the German guards honored our compound leader's request to make a special announcement. They then stood with us through the suggested full minute of reverent silence after the brief report that President Franklin Delano Roosevelt had died on the previous day.

I remembered other Germans in a boxcar south of Nuremberg who had snickered four months earlier while singing a ditty that appeared to ridicule Roosevelt, Churchill, and Stalin, and I wondered whether the guards' silence during this funereal minute now represented reverence or fear.

Next, the Germans installed a speaker above the door inside every room and piped music to us with occasional war news and commentary. We were surprised when we saw a crowd of kriegies gathering in our quadrangle and learned that the person it was forming around was a German! We soon heard he was Max Schmeling, a former world-champion boxer. Despite his purported remarks that he had just "dropped in to greet some of his good friends from America," we felt it was an obvious Kraut public relations ploy to influence our attitudes toward them; and we reminded ourselves that, until the war was officially declared over, we were still under the restrictions of "name, rank, and serial number only" orders.

Watching from the window of our room, we were incensed that the group following the German made it look as if the ploy was working. We consoled ourselves with calculations that the estimated crowd of under two hundred would be less than ten percent of the compound's total, that most of the crowd might be recent arrivals who hadn't seen the Germans' previous attitudes toward Americans as we had, and that at least no one from our room had the bad judgment to join in the following.

There was another report that still more food parcels had been received. Within days, we had gone from starvation rations to near the supplemental food quota intended and provided by the Red Cross. Though still cautiously conserving rations in case of some unforeseen change, we were slowly gaining strength. The mild weather of mid to late April helped increase the numbers of walkers along the perimeter.

The guards in the towers still fingered their guns, but some, especially the older ones among them, watched for upward glances from kriegies and took the opportunity to flash nervous smiles. The wisitors, as they had been dubbed, were becoming more comfortable on their occasional stops in the room. They managed to get responses to their attempts to converse in some of the rooms.

Once, when wisitors left our room after a short round of greetings, someone said, "I hear these guys are now saying that Nazis were the ones who really started the war; these guys are glad it's almost over because they never believed there should have been a war. The same ones that were kickin' us around a couple months ago now say they were really the good guys. How do you tell which is who?"

Someone else jested, "It'll be easy. When the war is over, we just kill all that's left, and everyone will agree there must have been some good guys among them, but nobody will care which ones were who."

Another cautioned seriously, "It won't be that easy." And yet another groaned, "Will that have to be our problem too?"

There was a consensus at this time that incarceration here could no longer extend into weeks — probably only into days. Waiting became increasingly exciting with anticipation of that glorious feeling "out there" called freedom. The purpose of perimeter walks changed from a way to pass the time to a way to rebuild our endurance for when we would "live" rather than merely wait. Interest in hobbies was replaced by curiosity about how liberation would occur.

We realized after lock-in one evening that, though we had spent four months with one another in very restricted quarters and had talked extensively about food, the war, Germans, and liberation, we knew little about one another's backgrounds or future hopes or dreams. When it appeared that no one cared about most of those things, someone suggested we at least each briefly tell his "horror story." He reminded us that that had all stopped when we had encountered the rule that there be no more "There-I-was-at-twenty-six-thousand-feet" talk.

We soon learned that there was little interest in discussing that subject either, but agreed we would poll room members to have each one say something personal or explain why he didn't want to.

One man among the twenty-four of us was not flying personnel. We knew only that he was "from the Medics," that he left to do volunteer work at the Stalag hospital each morning, and that he returned every evening to go quietly to sleep. He didn't want to talk. When we spoke favorably of the many hours he gave to those needing help, he called it "something to do." We had heard widely divergent comments about the hospital, from "good staff and services" to the opposite; he said all they had was "aspirins and bandages."

We insisted that his "horror story" would be unique to us because the only things we knew about were bailouts and crash landings. So he reluctantly mumbled that he was crossing a small river on a rather long and high footbridge to get to where medical help was needed. When he ran to the middle of the bridge, he saw "a bunch of Germans and bayonets and stuff coming on at the far end." He turned to run back and saw the same thing happening at the end he had just entered.

We thanked him heartily for his brief story; it was comforting to know that flying personnel weren't the only ones who got into embarrassing predicaments so easily. Someone suggested he talk loudly and proudly when he got home instead of mumbling as he just had done, and that he start the story with a bold catch-phrase like, "There I was at twenty-six feet."

Our bread-slicer agreed to say a few words about his preservice life as a tree topper for a firm that logged redwoods in northern California. To impress his new wife, he arranged to be at the tiptop of a tall tree when she came out one day to get him at the logging site.

"There I was at 260 feet," he explained, "when she asked my co-workers where I was. They pointed up and I waved down, but she wasn't impressed. She yelled, 'You get down here and don't ever go up that high again.'

Unfortunately, the Air Force didn't feel that order applied while I worked for them," he concluded.

A quiet and friendly roommate from whom we had heard only pleasant, positive words was urged to say more. He had never told his story to anyone: he didn't think anyone would believe it. When pressed, he said, "You've heard that nobody can get out of a centrifugal spin; I disproved that." They had lost part of a wing and other things, and he was pinned "like a frog on his belly" against the side in the waist as the plane dropped while dizzily whipping around and around and around. There was a large hole in the side of the plane several inches ahead of him; he thought he might live if he could get to the hole, and he knew he would die if he didn't. He didn't know he'd find his knees and palms and fingertips bloody later from struggling, and he kept slipping back while crawling forward. He "made progress like a caterpillar or maybe an earthworm."

When he reached the hole, the plane flung him out into space as if it had become annoyed with his persistence. He pulled the rip cord, and while the aircraft crashed in a deafening fireball a short distance away his chute snapped him upright in time to land among waiting Germans.

We had laughed at the clever images he created while comparing himself to a frog and a caterpillar, and we apologized for the seeming disrespect. He said he had enjoyed our laughter but didn't think he would tell the details when he got home: he didn't know another way to explain things, and he didn't want people to think it had been "more fun than a two-bit ride at the State Fair."

There were various other stories. I went to sleep remembering several acquaintances who hadn't survived, and realized that they had taken stories with them that were more horrifying than any.

We awoke to the grinding roar of aircraft engines laboring to gain altitude directly over our barracks. The Germans had run precariously low on gasoline to fuel their war machine months earlier, but now they had apparently drained last drops from all containers and were using repaired fighter-bombers to assist the efforts of ground forces.

The airfield near Barth, which had seldom been used in recent months, was now a launch strip for round-trips to the eastern front. We could identify markings on certain planes and time their flights.

Rumors were rampant. We knew the Russians had crossed the Oder and were on a revitalized dash toward the west, but we didn't know when it had happened, how much progress had been made after the crossing, or whether the assault might include a drive in our direction. Guesses were wildly optimistic. The most reliable information came from the front compounds, because the German guard force was talking to our internal headquarters. One of the reasons for that communication was an order from Berlin to evacuate the camp and move us toward the west. Our Colonel Zemke had declined.

Confirmation of details wasn't necessary to understand the outcome of that discussion. Our guards could control us with the machine-gun advantage from the towers, but they were not staffed to march over nine thousand troops without "grease guns" and the determination to use them. They had instead recently demonstrated that they now wished to be remembered as "nice guys" doing what they had been told to do. There was little point in moving us; there was no place to go, and the problem would recur within days if there were.

News and analysis from our room speakers had been replaced by beautiful classical music from renowned German composers. It seemed the "camp DJ" hoped we would remember that great creative people had come from their country. We knew that.

With only two days left in April, someone put up a sign that read, "O Happy Day, the First of May." We started hearing occasional explosions which seemed to be coming from Barth; we assumed that these resulted from demolition of items that local officials didn't want to be captured by Russians.

We heard that kriegies were digging foxholes in the older compounds. They had gotten shovels from the Germans, and they were also using tin cans from Red Cross parcels. The reasoning was that Russian ground troops who were headed our way could mistake our barracks arrangement for a German military encampment and shoot randomly toward us. The counter reasoning was that this was premature. As digging activities increased in other compounds, holes were started in our quadrangle by some who argued that it made "more sense to dig than die."

The frequency of explosions and excavations both increased on the last day of April. Toward evening, the shock wave from a gigantic blast shook our camp and sent everyone tumbling toward the nearest cover. I found myself on the floor against the wall of our room with others. Although temporarily somewhat deafened, we soon recovered to wonder what had happened. A glance toward the window revealed only that kriegies were crawling out from under barracks.

Realizing that our frail shelter offered little protection, we dashed outside and then saw that the building where the experimental radar work had been done was now only a cloud of debris in the sky. Tattered bits of asphalt roofing fluttered into our compound long after the explosion.

The best information we could confirm told us there had been no injuries; pieces large enough to cause damage hadn't hit anyone. There were comments like, "Fearless Fosdick will have to find another job now," and, "They'll be able to hang the left-over tinsel on the Christmas tree next winter."

Despite attempts to sound casual, however, there was an underlying fear of similar unknowns yet to come that might threaten our safety. We slept uneasily. As the first dim light seemed to be changing the darkness to dawn, a couple of roommates returned from the night latrine whispering excitedly to each other. Then others whispered to them from their bunks. Suddenly, everyone was whispering loudly:

"The Germans are gone!"

We crowded to the window and strained our eyes to confirm that the men in the towers were kriegies with large white handkerchiefs tied around an upper arm. Our barrack door was still barred, but there was another kriegie with an armband walking across the quadrangle: obviously, there were no dogs!

The speaker above our door then crackled; a novice operator was apparently trying to check in; it crackled again. Finally: "Good morning, men. This is Colonel Zemke, your senior officer speaking."

No one would remember all of his words verbatim, but everyone listening would forever remember the excitement of hearing him. The German guard force had contacted him the previous evening to say they would abandon the camp during the night and travel westward to submit to American forces.

As the ranking officer, it was his military duty to assume command and retain order. He felt personally responsible for our well-being and he hoped that, when contact with the American Military was reestablished, he could report that we had all acted faithfully.

He told us the men in the towers were scouts who would remain there until communication with the Russians had been assured. Radio attempts to contact the Russian Military were in progress, and messengers in abandoned German military vehicles carrying white flags were now traveling toward the eastern front.

He thanked all those who were working and all who had volunteered and said others might be asked to work later, but there was presently an overabundance of help. He said he knew we would want to wander outside the fences to begin to reestablish the feeling of freedom or simply the feeling of the green grass beyond the perimeter. For these purposes, all gates of our camp, between compounds and to the outside world, were open.

He explained that we could all think of ourselves as an advance outpost, waiting for orders in the northernmost tip of Germany, and he was sure we would represent our country favorably. He added that he did not wish to impose restrictive military rules but asked us to stay within the immediate area and retain the camp's status quo, all of which would expedite the start of our trip home.

The colonel concluded with the assurance that he would keep us informed, and the speaker crackled again.

Formerly pent-up emotions now distorted expressions, and tears ran across twisted smiles. Finally, it was all right to cry — and it was all right to laugh; many seemed to be doing both at the same time as we exchanged handshakes around the room and thumped one another's shoulders.

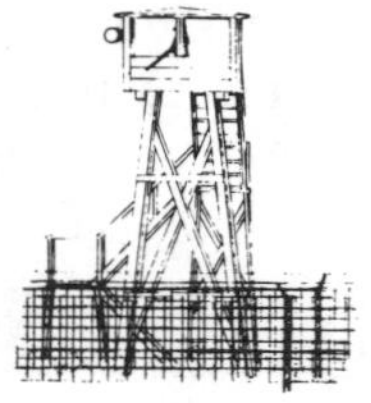

Chapter 14

Trouble Ahead

Emotional pandemonium was rampant everywhere after Colonel Zemke's announcement that we were free. There was also a feeling of security with the colonel's declared leadership role, and we accepted his suggestions to retain current behavior patterns for our immediate well-being.

Many were cautious as they made plans to visit the local outside world. I didn't wish merely to rush through the gate; I wanted the initial exit to feel ceremonious so I could savor the memory later.

On my way to the gate, I made a short stop at the day-latrine and was startled by the first of various bizarre incidents I would witness during the liberation experience. The urinal, which was similar to a huge galvanized sheet metal rain gutter one foot wide and deep and ten feet long, this morning had its inside surfaces randomly covered with large glossy prints of the stern and determined gaze of Germany's Fuhrer.

Others who entered the latrine chuckled with surprise as I had, and one cheerily said, "Well, good morning, Adolf," as he urinated on one of the photographs. Curious, I made a fast check on my way out, and noticed more of the same prints at the bottom of all of the straddle stalls. Along the path outside, a stick pinned one of the photos to the ground, distorting the facial features into a wince.

There must have been stacks of those prints in the abandoned guard office awaiting the day of victory for the Third Reich.

I walked out to the unsurfaced roadway that ran along the fence just outside our compound. The grass looked too fresh and fragile and precious to be trampled, so I first paced along the dusty path. Deciding that I should discard such feelings and recover a normal attitude toward nature, I strayed diagonally into the field for many yards before pivoting to stop and look back.

The drab fences and barracks and the people milling about inside looked exactly as I'd expected, except that it all seemed far away. I was momentarily frightened about my mental well-being because it also all seemed long ago: it was like the evil events in a scary dream from which one struggles to awaken; once fully conscious, one realizes that the bad things never happened. I felt that I must now make a special effort to remember everything.

Thousands of men were moving about inside the compound and hundreds were testing their liberty outside the fences. I took a short walk to a small wooded area nearby. Several others were strolling about examining the trees. I saw a man defecating, and then another, and another. This seemed indecent, but I soon realized we were as sheltered from outsiders here on the side of the camp away from Barth as we were in our latrine; this was merely another expression of freedom: these men had decided they would never use that filthy place again.

I circled back to the compound. Sure that freedom could now be anywhere, I wished to get an update on news. The airfield at Barth had been extensively mined by departing Germans. Zemke wanted it cleared so planes of the Eighth Air Force from England could use the strip to evacuate us as soon as their war assignments were concluded. An abundance of anxious volunteers was already working on it.

Reports on current progress of the war could be heard frequently on room speakers directly from the BBC in London. Just as there had been over nine hundred navigators available to make maps, there were over nine hundred radio operator/mechanics who knew how to rig connections for the messages that everyone now wanted to hear.

News commentators indicated difficulty in sorting facts from assumptions. Russian military forces continued to destroy what was left of Berlin during the battle that had already raged for ten days. The four American armies and one French, one British, and one Canadian army, all under Eisenhower, seemed to be idly waiting along the Elbe River some fifty miles to the west. They were, however, continually accepting the surrender of Germans fleeing from the east.

The remaining strip of Germany and its government appeared to be mostly in chaos. There was a report that Hitler had died on the previous day, probably from suicide. But he had left an order to save Berlin at any cost and to "drown the Russians in a sea of blood."

Although radio news indicated that the war would end somehow and soon, our immediate concern was successful contact and communication with those Russians headed toward us. Since that effort was already in progress, we turned our attention to internal interests.

There were rumors, confirmed later, that German civilians, mostly women (because all able-bodied men had gone west) were begging in and around gate areas of the front compounds.

Many of the older ones, the "fraus," mostly wanted food. They had heard we received and stored food from the Red Cross; some tended to be domineering and demanded that we share. Because of the open gates, hundreds of parcels had reportedly been lost to those who grabbed boxes and walked out before an affirmative policy against their looting could be enforced.

Most of the younger ones, the "fraulines," also wanted food, but even more they wanted American males to take home with them. Their reasons became obvious after a few hints: a Russian would bypass their house if he noticed the place was occupied by an Allied soldier. They were terrified that "the barbarians" would otherwise kick in their doors, rape them, and then murder them. Obviously, they had analyzed their immediate future in more detail than we had ours, and the days ahead proved there was considerable accuracy in their forecasts.

The fraulines made enticing suggestions. They acknowledged their money had no value, but they felt they could offer a luxuriant life compared to that in our quarters, with the addition of more variety and freedom than most servicemen could expect after returning to the States. Many former kriegies left with the fraulines, indicating they would return when they saw American planes circling the airfield.

Someone in our group noted that, with the war still in progress, those who left were "fraternizing with the enemy." Others reasoned that we had no roll call, no morning report, no military police: under those conditions there's always a small percentage willing to defect temporarily.

To lighten the discussion, someone else in our group changed two of the words in Elizabeth Browning's poem and facetiously misquoted the opening lines: "Why do I love thee? Let me count the reasons."

The facts about the inception and operation of the POW WOW could now be known, as there was no longer a need to protect it. Much of the story had been quite accurately anticipated by most former kriegies. Early in the history of the camp, the clandestine organization of traders, who were called "interpreters" to conceal their secret mission, purchased radio circuit components from guards. The price was American cigarettes from Red Cross parcels. Parts were bought one at a time from different guards so each German could reason that whatever was being planned probably wouldn't work. Costs varied widely but were always high; several cartons were paid for each of the main components.

Construction was accomplished by some of the ten percent in the camp who were service-trained radio operator/mechanics, and the completed receiver was hidden in the wall of the office where the Germans had prisoners compile, summarize, and type the camp's roll-call reports.

After condensing the BBC news, the "editors" made a copy for each barrack on the office typewriters. On rare occasions when carbon paper supplies ran low, other paper was "carbonized" over a smoky vegetable-oil fire in a barrack stove. We recalled that the POW WOW had been very difficult to read at times.

Copies for each barrack had to be distributed to the other compounds before evening lockup. But who could be expected to pass through the gates without at least occasional frisking? The chaplains, of course; men of the cloth were always glad to carry the good news without telling the wrong people!

Although many former prisoners still seemed unsure of the reality of freedom, open gates everywhere encouraged exploration of other compounds. Some visited crew members they had been separated from here, and others attempted to relocate friends they had lost contact with before arrival at Stalag Luft I.

I was surprised, during a short return to the room, to find a small picture of myself staring back from an ID card on my sleeping pad. A couple of roommates had been at the main guard office the Germans had abandoned; when they saw a crowd of kriegies pulling Kgf cards from files, they took those that belonged to others in our room.

Mental readjustments were necessary again because it seemed like a lifetime since we had heard, "Undt now luke at Meekey Mouse undt laugh. . . ."

Other reported discoveries from the office area temporarily sobered us. A filed copy of a February communique from Hitler ordered that all of us be shot and cremated and that ashes be mailed to home addresses with a note saying this would only partially avenge the bombing of Dresden. Two months before we noticed a change in the guards' attitudes, they were already disobeying orders from their Fuhrer because of fear of ultimate vengeance.

We saw a small Russian scouting party crossing a distant field that afternoon. There was not the excitement we had anticipated, as initial identification was by elimination only: there were no other military movements within miles. Rumors from the front compounds claimed that communication with "Uncle Joe's men" had been established.

Radio news the following day told us Berlin had fallen. There wasn't much left to shoot at, no fire was being returned, so the Russians hung their red flag on the Reichstag building. This flag had a hammer and sickle instead of a white circle with a swastika. It couldn't have been that simple for anyone in Berlin, but that seemed to be the gist of what was being reported; it didn't mean the war had ended. There was still sporadic fighting in resistance pockets along the remaining strip of Germany, and no one had officially surrendered for the country.

That afternoon brought Russians into our camp. Word of their arrival at the front compounds preceded the appearance of several of them in our area. Initial meetings were overtly demonstrative with boisterous greetings of "Rooski, Amerikonski, comradski." That much was mutually understood and respected. Unfortunately, oral communication stopped totally after those three words; further understanding was nil.

Exaggerated pantomime with much gesturing threatened respect when misunderstood. Their sighting out over extended arms, slashing with index fingers, and wincing while thrusting fingers into their bellies, told us they had shot, bayoneted, and slit throats of many Germans. Had we? No? Their disbelieving expressions questioned our value.

A couple of our communicators bent over, spread arms widely, and waddled around trying to look like airplanes to the perplexed Russians. Someone near the back of our little group revived one of our inter-branch Service gibes: "Gravel grinders never do understand fly boys." That brought chuckles from Americans, but the chuckles brought glaring suspicion from the Russians. One of us raised the "Rooski, Amerikonski, comradski" chant to reestablish our alliance.

Some Russians wandered toward other areas, while two who remained drew outlines of their tank treads to tell us they drove tanks. Their tanks were huge. We knew; our country had supplied them. They didn't know that, and we were unable to explain where their tanks had come from.

Their tanks could push down big barracks as fragile as ours. We knew that too. They would get their tanks and demonstrate. No! Our closed eyes and tilted heads with cheeks pressed against praying hands were meant to say we had to sleep there until we went home. Unfortunately, that made us look more like pansies than soldiers. The Russians didn't approve of our rejection of their offer — they slept under their tanks! There was, no doubt, some kind of trouble ahead.

By now it was night and time to sleep. But life, and the anticipation of going home, had become too good to miss in sleeping. Our new disc jockeys were piping the clear sweet sounds of music from recent American Hit Parades over our speakers. There were preferences among some listeners, but we all liked all of it. If it hadn't been true, we probably would have pretended it was.

We hadn't heard most of the songs before and one of them seemed almost too appropriate. A forgotten sound — a lovely voice — the heavenly voice of a human female who had never had to consider losing her freedom, joyfully lilted in true western style, a song that became an instant favorite. I hummed it repeatedly throughout the night, but in my ecstasy I could remember only a few of the words:

Don't fence me in,
Let me ride,

O'er the wide
Open country that I love.
Don't fence me in.

Russian soldiers were coming into our area from all directions on the third morning after contact. There was no longer a visible enemy separating the East from the West. The raucous greeting of "Rooski, Amerikonski, comradski" could be heard almost continuously. Language problems should have been diminishing somewhat; while we weren't able to interpret disapproval until feelings were hurt, we now knew the difference between "da" and "nyet." As more contacts were made, it became easier to find a person who could translate occasional words and redirect understanding.

Mistrust, however, remained an obvious deterrent to any sincere friendliness. Days later, after we had all been separated again, Americans reasoned that misunderstandings of cultural differences had been more detrimental than language barriers.

Americans measured military seniority by time served: we could all readily quote the date of our induction into the service and the number of months expired since. Dates and time meant little or nothing to the Russians; they cited having entered the fighting at Chinsk, or some other place that meant nothing to us. So we couldn't compare merits as soldiers.

Our laughter commonly followed true joy or harmless humor; they more often used laughter as ridicule. Therefore, they frequently thought we were laughing at them instead of with them.

As we later analyzed the few days we had been together, we remembered their egocentricity: the greeting had always been "Rooski, Amerikonski, comradski." We had never gotten first mention.

They appeared unaware of intricate and complicated systems that we used to estimate or compare material values. A nineteen-year-old gunner among us was distraught because a demanding Russian, with a decoration he had taken from a German uniform, forced a trade for the gunner's expensive wristwatch. The watch had been a high school graduation present from his parents the previous year, and it was one of the few that had survived all German searches.

There were various stories about Russian tempers being piqued by rejections of offers of German military trinkets for Americans' wedding rings. A few explained how angry Russians had threatened to help remove rings with drawn military knives when enlarged knuckles were a problem.

We found ourselves perplexed and whispering to each other, "They're acting like savages." But we felt it might only be a lack of understanding, because, after they learned we had been hungry while the Germans failed to provide food, they herded forty pigs into our camp from neighboring area farms. When some of the pigs ran through our compound, we amused ourselves with questions of whether these were replacements for the police dogs.

Now we whispered, "Are they barbarians like the Jerries told us they were?" We reasoned, however, that they were merely doing things that way because they were from a different culture.

That evening they entertained us, or maybe they just enjoyed themselves in front of the captive audience we provided. One of them played a kind of harmonica in the quadrangle while several others danced around him, or, at least, bounced around with bent knees. Some frequently yelped musical-type noises while bouncing. A few of them did handstands and cartwheels.

A performance they seemed most enthusiastic about was one in which a dancer held another by the wrists, swinging him around horizontally through several circles, and then releasing him to bounce on the ground and roll to a stop many yards away. They seemed pleased that we were amazed at their lusty gymnastics.

We slept uneasily again, wondering what the outcome of our interrelationships might be. Colonel Zemke interrupted the programming on our speakers in the morning to put us on military alert for a possible immediate move. His explanation was very diplomatic, though necessarily sketchy.

In essence, the Russians mistrusted us. We had neither killed Germans nor destroyed German property in the days since the guards had left. We hadn't even been to Barth, but we had allowed those enemies to come and take food from us. These were some of the reasons for Russian suspicions, but they had other concerns.

The men of the Second White Russian Army were clearly the conquerors of this area, yet some of the Americans hadn't even appeared submissive or cooperative. In brief summary: they wished to move us. They were armed; we weren't.

Their plan would take us a thousand miles southeast across Poland and Russia to the port of Odessa on the Black Sea. We would walk the first one hundred miles. "Russian military trucks," which we knew to be American lend-lease equipment, would then take us the remaining distance from around Stettin or Berlin. Rail transportation over part of the way "could also be a possibility." American ships could then come in through the Mediterranean, Aegean, and Black seas to get us. Zemke wanted us to be ready, but he was objecting; rather, "negotiating" — he had to go.

We worried. Their plan was barely plausible. We had not yet recovered adequately since our starvation period to walk a hundred miles in four or five days. From there, the trip by truck would take several more days on their roads. We had no equipment to carry food. Arrangements to get ships to Odessa could take many weeks.

With no Rooskis in the compound this morning, we could commiserate freely among ourselves. Did we trust the Russians? Once on their trucks, would we be taken to Odessa?

The speakers crackled again after lunch. Zemke had compared the simplicity of our plan to the complexity of theirs, but our comparisons didn't concern them. Their suspicion remained: "Why had we placidly sat there?" Because we were unarmed, he had told them, we waited for them to secure the area; with their approval, we would now be happy to celebrate their victory with them.

The colonel acknowledged our desire to save the barracks for our own use, and even for subsequent use by a multitude of now displaced persons in Europe. But no one would need fences or guard towers. Tear them down jubilantly, he suggested, then go to Barth and celebrate with the Rooskis, act like Rooskis — just be back by dark in case this new twist in our plan didn't convince them. He would tell them he had now given permission for this, and he would continue negotiating.

Everyone reacted according to his own feelings. A few just sat stunned, but most ran with yodels and war whoops to the fence on the side toward Barth. Our world went crazy. As thousands of liberated kriegies yelled and swayed on the fence, the posts cracked and then snapped over like dominoes for the length of the camp.

We couldn't tell laughter from tears again as the din increased. With the fence down, many started toward Barth while others brought saws and axes from the maintenance area to destroy guard towers. With twenty men chopping and sawing and pushing under each tower, it was time to yell "timber" within minutes and then stand back to watch as the towers toppled and glass that had protected guards from cold winter winds now shattered among the weeds.

From a sense of duty, I joined the obstreperous stream of humanity headed across the short mile of fields toward Barth. I felt uneasy about the crowd's abandonment of reason, but I didn't want to sit and stare uselessly.

Within minutes, we could see the sun's reflections glisten from the shimmering horizon of the Baltic Sea to our left. I stepped away from the mainstream of walkers. A panorama of blue from the sea blended into the verdant variations of the earth. I was enthralled: here, away from the fetid odors of the camp, balmy breezes off the Baltic wafted sweet scents from the grasses and wildflowers and weeds. I hadn't remembered life could be this good.

Others stopped momentarily and then rejoined the crowd. As I ambled farther from the path, I overheard, "The guy is probably looking for birds." Fortunately, no one cared about my leaving. I continued down the small incline and was soon out of sight. I was now sure; I wanted to be alone. I trotted up onto another little ridge overlooking the water. I could no longer hear the babbling from the groups headed toward Barth.

A wagon track followed the shoreline below the slope ahead of me, and a flat gray rock appeared to jut out into the bay. I would stand on the rock and enjoy hearing only the gentle lapping of the water.

Delighted with all the beauty, I skipped down the slope like a child. But something was very wrong with the flat rock. As it came into focus, it was at the water's edge, but it was high and narrow. It had wheels. It was a baby buggy. It faced the bay and there were human bodies on the ground extending back into the path.

I felt bewitched by some evil spirit while walking slowly forward to stand near the buggy. The bodies of four women lay on their backs, each neatly clothed in dresses fashioned from pieces of military uniform material.

Their ages were roughly twenty, forty, sixty, and eighty. Five generations, I thought, although my guess might have been wrong; the two in the middle could have been sisters. Each of them had a bullet-hole through both temples, and a Mauser rifle lay on the ground at the head of the oldest.

The youngest lay next to the buggy. Her right hand was now relaxed between the spokes of a wheel, but creases in the palm showed that her grip had been intense while the rifle recoiled.

I back-stepped to glance into the buggy. Scraps of pink cloth puckered into little rosettes decorated the white flannel blanket. I was amazed at the amount of blood that had drained from such a tiny head. A pool the size of a saucer had dried to red, purple, and brown stains.

Each of the other mothers' right hands had gripped her daughter's left shoulder in the diagonal arrangement away from the buggy. At the top of the line lay the scowling matriarch, her mouth gaping open in a twisted oval. My mind shouted, "You old bitch, you killed them all!" Another part of my mind immediately apologized. Germans were very deliberate and methodic; these four had agreed that for these five, this was best. I wondered if I had shouted aloud.

I remembered someone in the compound that morning asking if there was work to be done. As usual, there was an abundance of volunteers. Another had answered, "There's five Jerry broads to be dug under, but Zemke wants 'em left for one more day in case they got kin that might claim the bodies." That seemed right.

I tried to say a prayer, but I couldn't think of any words. The quiet was frightening. I could now hear only the gentle lapping of the water.

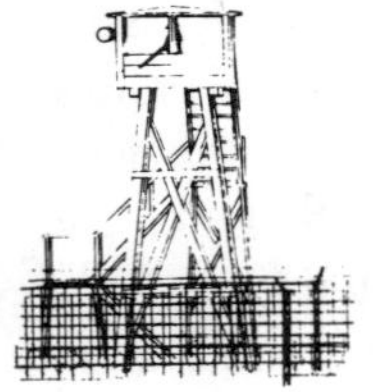

Chapter 15

That Thin Line on the Horizon

The track along the water's edge no doubt circled into Barth, but I didn't wish to see wild victory celebrations in the city after my chance encounter with the suicide scene.

I pondered the plight of German civilians while climbing the grade back toward our barracks. They had little space left after Hitler's terse orders not to yield "even so much as a millimeter." Those who had survived bombings would now face the fury of Russian ground forces. I had never doubted the Germans' fear; I just hadn't realized the intensity of it.

Noises from the ridge were more raucous now than when I had left the path. Former prisoners were now going in both directions. Most of those returning from Barth were carrying things: pots, pans, clocks, pillows. . . .

I felt somewhat distressed by sounds of reveling coming from the barracks, and I entered our room quietly, still dazed from the waterfront experience. A white bundle hit my chest. My arms cupped to catch it as someone cheered, "You was just issued your sheets, buddy. Remember sheets?" I didn't at first. "Man, have they got a quartermaster in Barth," the voice continued, "They got more of everything than the Air Force ever thought of. Them Rooskis is kickin' in doors."

Someone pushed me forward, jesting, "Look at the monkey, fella. Remember mirrors?" A large mirror hung beside our door. "Smile for the monkey. Remember that guy?" I wasn't sure. I was temporarily shocked.

Most had refrained from bringing things because they realized space in the room would be a problem. But many had brought pillows: two or three pillows arranged lengthwise served as a luxurious mattress without encroaching on bunkmates' areas.

Stories of experiences with the Russians became exhausting as others returned from Barth. Americans who had entered residences in town were generally reminded of civilian conveniences at home, but most Russians had not yet been in homes west of the Oder and were intrigued by the gadgets. Common entertainment for Americans had been watching bewildered Rooskis flush washcloths down toilets and then race to the basement in an attempt to relocate the washcloth.

One Russian had been pleased with the scent of toothpaste after removing the cap from a tube he found in a bathroom. He squeezed the entire contents onto a slice of black bread in the kitchen and seemed delighted as he devoured his snack.

Some had successfully learned to operate toasters and cameras, but others tried to toast bread in cameras, or take pictures with toasters.

Similar stories continued to the point of boredom.

That evening brought tentatively good news: Russian leaders were softening toward accepting our original plan. We went to sleep hearing murmurs of ecstatic pleasure from those who had acquired pillow-mattresses.

We learned the terms of the agreement regarding our immediate future when we awoke in the morning. We would remain at Stalag Luft I until the Eighth Air Force picked us up from the Barth air strip, but the Russians would cordon off the peninsula with armed sentries as the German guards had done when an escape was suspected. Were we now prisoners of our allies? We didn't care. We had more area than we could use in the few days remaining.

There were other rules: visits to Barth would continue, but in groups of twenty to thirty with one member designated as a responsible leader. Because many had not returned to camp after the previous day, we accepted the tightened restrictions as a consequence of that lack of self-discipline.

I joined one of the many groups that formed for a walk into Barth. We already knew the town was a mostly residential one, with eleven thousand people, and we didn't expect this to be a sightseeing adventure. But many of us would never forget the conditions that we hadn't realized would be the civilians' penalties for losing a war.

A natural opening question as we entered a street of neat homes was, "Why are all the doors standing open?" Oh yes, it was a way to save doors — we remembered when we saw some that were cracked and broken: the Rooskis never opened doors; they always kicked them in.

Our group ambled along a narrow street between straight rows of well-kept wood-frame houses. "Hometown Germany" could have been any modest "Hometown USA," except, "Why was everyone standing out on their front lawns?" Oh yes, it was safer. They could be badly hurt or killed if they were inside and acted inappropriately when someone walked through and took something; but out here they could pretend they owned nothing. I remembered our lead guard in Vienna telling us never to respond to questions, to look tired, and to look only at the ground. Now it was their turn.

But these were housewives, with a few old men and a few frightened children. We hadn't been fighting these people!

There was no strict accounting of names and numbers among the Americans, and if someone paused or straggled, he merely joined a similar group in the area. The few remaining Russians moved about as they pleased, singly or in pairs. Calls of "Rooski, Amerikonski, comradski" had been replaced by wary nods which everyone hoped were intended and interpreted as acknowledgment of respect.

I noticed a woman look furtively over her shoulder when someone walked into the house behind her. Except for a brief glance, she ignored him when he came out minutes later carrying a small radio. Several seconds later, her face crumpled into the apron her hands brought up from her waist, but only briefly. After a few deft wipes, it came up dry to stare stoically in another direction.

There were many similar scenes. A palsied nod kept an old man's head bobbing slightly as his hands gripped two picket tips of a white wooden fence. Someone had no doubt yelled the German equivalent of "Go stand in the front yard, Grandpa, so they don't kill you." He appeared to be a kindly man, and when I got directly in front of him I stopped and said, "Gooten Morgan."

He had probably seen everything in his eighty years, except hordes of different kinds of enemies walk down the streets and through his home. Possibly he had fought in Germany's first world war, but that had ended twenty-seven years earlier. Now mute, he stared, but appeared to see nothing. A tiny tear-track glistened from each eye to the corners of his gaping mouth, and his head continued bobbing.

After a circuitous trip through Barth we walked out to an impoundment of political prisoners of the Nazis. Because there was little or no other competent help in the area, volunteer medics from our camp were directing other volunteers in evacuation and cleanup.

Conditions here seemed to be as bad as rumors had indicated. Prisoners had been worked until too feeble, then left to die, and finally dragged to a space below the living quarters by surviving prisoners. There were various nationalities including German, but most, reportedly, were French.

Wires surrounding the area were equipped with insulators and had been electrically charged. Volunteer workers were wearing masks. We didn't wish to see any more details unless we could assist, and they couldn't use additional help; so we returned to our barrack.

At our camp we learned that one American casualty had occurred since liberation: a kriegie in another compound had repeatedly commented over many previous months that he could consume the entire contents of a Red Cross parcel in one sitting, and that, when conditions permitted, he would. He had — and then he died. In a coincidental situation on the same day another kriegie had become very ill while eating to fulfill a similar promise. He retracted his boast and survived.

We learned that two former German wisitors who had been known to be helping our side of the cause for months had remained when the other guards left and were given American clothes to protect them from the Russians. Most kriegies seemed pleased, assuming the Americans were sure these had proved to be "good guys."

I met someone from my former high school who had heard that still another former resident of our home town was interned at Stalag Luft I. After finding the third man, we took a short walk to discuss the odds of three previous occupants of a village of only eight hundred people becoming interned together in a prisoner-of-war camp six thousand miles away.

We agreed that we would each probably return to the village only to visit. That seemed to be the sole item of common interest among us; we were reminded of the line from the World War I song, "How ya gonna keep 'em down on the farm?"

With tools and material and freedom, there were interesting ways for everyone to pass time. Some just rested, but most were active. Many made rafts from our broken-down fence posts, and others made boats with lumber from the demolished towers.

Successful products were carried to bays on the Baltic for offshore touring. A small group that had ventured to an island returned with a harrowing story of being shot at several times by Russian guards from the sentry line. Impacts of the bullets were widely dispersed because they had been fired from "a mile away," but a few had splattered water within several yards of their boat.

Many former prisoners enjoyed drinking the fresh milk they took from tame cows abandoned on the peninsula. City boys who learned how to extract milk were pleased with their newly acquired capability, but were puzzled later when it no longer worked. Country boys were then delighted to explain, "Ya can't expect to get milk from 'em every five minutes around the clock. Ya gotta rest 'em fer a couple hours at least now and then so's they can make more."

We learned from radio broadcasts on the seventh of May that a German general had crawled from the rubble to sign papers which the Allies would consider an official unconditional surrender. That announcement might not have been fair to the magnitude of what had finally been accomplished, but it quite accurately described everyone's attitude toward Germany's ability to defend what little was left.

We heard later that either the seventh or eighth of May would be declared "V-E Day" to commemorate victory in Europe, and that wild celebrations had broken out in cities all across America.

We had mixed feelings; we were glad they were joyous, but wished they could have waited for us, at the same time remembering that celebrations could never include everyone. There were already predictions that American military personnel would be coming and going to and from Europe for months or maybe years to keep the peace.

While we discussed whether and how we should celebrate, someone started a fire near the edge of the camp. That was it. Fenceposts were carried until our bonfire was "big as a house," and it was kept burning until the wee hours of morning.

Clearing the mines from the airfield at Barth was completed, and the Eighth Air Force had been notified. They had known about us. Cargo planes in England were being readied, and B-17 bombers were being stripped so they could transport more personnel per trip; there were ninety thousand prisoners of war to be collected from all over Germany.

Everything was ready. Impatient men waited quietly to preclude any delay of whatever the evacuation procedure would be. There was nothing to talk about and there was no need to talk. Everyone seemed happy, but the repressed anticipation was intense. We waited through the day, and the next, and the next.

Typical humor of that time was to sit mute and motionless until someone whispered one more time, "You think they'll come tomorrow?" and then leap up yelling, "Calm down, dammit. They'll come when everything's ready."

A cheer on the morning of the twelfth of May told us planes were approaching. Initial sightings were more exhilarating than anything any of us could remember: it was good to see loose formations unconcerned about attacks from enemy fighters.

Evacuation would start with the front compounds. First in would be first out; that seemed fair. Planes landed, loaded, and left all day long. The routine continued the following morning. Before lunch, we could see groups leaving from the adjacent compound, and our turn for the exciting walk to the airstrip came in the early afternoon.

We were counted into the huge belly of a C-46 cargo plane. There were no parachutes; this was scary for airmen who had always carried them and had learned their value on previous flights. We sat on the floor and jostled against each other on our trip down the runway, but everyone took a chance at crowding in for a last view from a window as we banked gently into a turn toward the west.

Then we all agreed that we didn't know why we had looked — we hadn't wanted to see the place again.

The plane took us down to circle Cologne for an aerial view of rubble that the pilot considered typical results of British and American efforts to win the war. We appreciated his gesture but were more interested in seeing whatever our destination was to be.

We landed at Laon, France, and reloaded to GI trucks for a thirty-mile ride south to Reims. Waiting C-47's flew us to Le Havre, and trucks took us through the city and on to Fécamp, twenty miles to the north, overlooking the English Channel.

In our ride over the French countryside, we could see why the Allies had won the war: countless rows of closely parked American tanks stood in a large field that rolled out of sight into a valley; a similar field down the road was filled with trucks, another with jeeps, then half-tracks — and the scenes were repeated over and over. Where would they now find the land to grow the crops to feed Europe?

In our ride through Le Havre we could see another reason the Allies had won the war: Cologne had been heavily bombed, but this French seaport had been hit from land, sea, and air. Awestruck, I tried to think of phrases that might describe the areas we viewed from the high platform of a GI truck. I remembered from home gigantic windrows of snow that had been pushed to the sides of a road by a tractor after a huge midwestern blizzard. Windrows we sped between for miles here were similar, except these consisted of bricks and stones and chunks of masonry.

Several blocks away to our left and right, our trucks were speeding in the opposite direction; between the few cleared streets were only broken building foundations and everything that had collapsed among them. Where would they now put the people of Europe who needed shelter?

American vehicles were the only means of transportation in this part of France; that was the way it had been in Italy six months before. The trucks took us to one of several tent cities set up to receive former prisoners of war. Each of the tent areas was named after a popular brand of American cigarettes; ours was called Camp Lucky Strike.

We held our breath and closed our eyes while passing through heavy fumes and vapors of disinfectant tents; we laughed and sang through shower tents; we gleefully accepted shaving kits and similar goodies, donned new uniforms, and enjoyed fresh haircuts.

Meals in the assigned mess tents were limited to light servings with little or no salt or sugar for the first week. Seasonings were added and portions increased in the second week, sugared desserts were included in the third, and then varieties and amounts became like holiday meals.

The cautious diets may not have been necessary for returnees like ourselves, whose food intake had increased in recent weeks, but the efforts were respected as a good average approach to rehabilitating tens of thousands of former prisoners from widely varied conditions pouring in from all over Europe daily.

We had lost track of crew mates, roommates, and even camp mates, but that caused no concern; we met new tent mates and had no desire to discuss recent pasts. It was like a re-induction, except that we discussed what our return to the States might be like.

Competitive spirits were rekindled in communal card games in various tents, but many of us preferred long walks over the rural countryside. We found the French sincerely friendly and apparently appreciative of our presence. We learned to say, "Bone-sjur, Mess-uere, coma sa va," to the farmers; we didn't know what that meant, but it always brought smiles. Farmers' wives enjoyed something about our attempts to call them "Mam-zel."

An option to the wait for the boat in France was offered in the form of a thirty-day furlough in England; we would then report to a designated shipping point there after the leave. We appreciated the offer, but few took it, partly because those formerly from "the Eighth" said, "Why should I miss the boat from here because I'm eating fish 'n chips on Piccadilly?"

Curious about an outbreak of excitement, I joined a run toward a gathering crowd one morning. "They're U.S. Congressmen, but nobody knows which ones," was the first message as we caught glimpses of civilian suits and hats and topcoats. Then, "It's Ike! It's Ike! It's Eisenhower!" circulated through the crowd, as the hemisphere's leading uniformed hero made his way into our mob. He moved slowly along nodding and smiling, and stopped at every tenth soldier to ask where he had been and how things were.

His arrival was not totally unexpected, because there was a mike and speaker at the makeshift platform to which the General climbed to express thanks for our "help in the world's most massive effort ever to reestablish freedom and justice."

As we returned to the tents after he left, someone said, "Those dudes in the suits almost got trampled trying to find out what's happening over here now that everything is safely settled."

As our fourth week was ending, the trucks picked us up for a ride to a loading dock in Le Havre, where we boarded a ship named *Excelsior*. She was being overloaded to transport the most troops possible, as had been promised; we slept on bunks or decks wherever there was room, glad to be going in the right direction regardless of conditions.

England loomed large and gray but distant in the fog toward the starboard as we left the Channel. With some impatience, we nicknamed our ship "the Straw-bottom," even though the trip was to take only one-fourth the time that the eighty-two-ship convoy had taken.

Congestion from troops returning through the New York harbors caused a change in routing plans after three days at sea, and we were redirected southward to the Newport News area. On the eighth morning, that thin line on the horizon reappeared where I had left it almost nine months earlier.

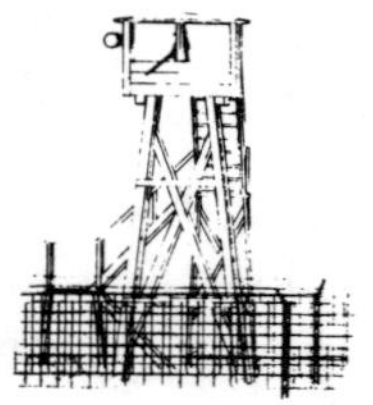

Chapter 16

Was It Fair?

Queues of returned servicemen lined up for over a block at all phone booths around the clock on the base at Camp Patrick Henry, Virginia. After waiting three days for arrangements, I boarded a troop train to Ft. Sheridan, near Chicago. I nervously dropped the required coins into a telephone box when I arrived there and waited for my parents' neighbor to answer the call. Like many others from that era, my parents had saved phone expenses since the '29 depression through message arrangements with a friendly neighbor.

The man was elderly with poor hearing and a faulty memory, but he said they had worried about me, my parents were well, he would tell them I had called and expected to be home the following day.

The train stopped at the center of the village only long enough for me to step clear. I shouldered my flight bag, passed the few stores, and walked the four blocks to my parents' home at the edge of the village.

Nothing had changed. Everything was quiet and untouched by the sordid facts of the other worlds. I waved a greeting to a lady hanging laundry in her back yard and was sure she wondered "whose boy" that was, coming home on furlough.

I could see my mother working in an outdoor flowerbed when I neared the lot line. She directed a confused stare toward me after I cheerily called, "Hi, Mom," she burst into sobs while I approached, and she cried uncontrollably when I helped her into the house. Then she tearfully recounted the dates and occasions of her emotional ordeal as I listened sympathetically through the few hours until my father and sister returned from their work day.

During the morning of the previous third of January, the minister had driven into the yard, followed by the car with my father and sister, and finally, the postmaster. Her mind had gone blank with fear knowing something must be wrong, especially when she noticed my sister was crying.

The postmaster read a telegram addressed to her:

> The Secretary of War desires me to express his deep regret that your son Corporal Melvin G. TenHaken has been reported missing in action since sixteen December over Italy. If further details or other information are received you will be promptly notified.

She had filed the copy of the telegram in a large cardboard box that contained all newspaper clippings, cards, letters, and other documents received since I had entered the Service.

A letter from the War Department arrived several days after the telegram to explain details reported by other airmen on our mission. It said our plane "dropped out of formation and began to lose altitude," and that "seven parachutes were observed to emerge from this aircraft before it disappeared into an undercast." Those reporting had apparently been unable to see the eighth chute from their angle in the then-distant formation.

The War Department's letter included a list of the eleven names and next-of-kin home addresses of those who had been on the plane; that list started written communications between all crew members' families.

A smiling postmaster had pounded on the door on St. Valentine's day with a copy of another telegram, this one with what he called the "good news" that the missing son was a prisoner of war in Germany. Over forty letters and postcards arrived in subsequent days from people, mostly amateur radio operators, who monitored shortwave broadcasts and also heard the Germans' enumeration of those recently captured.

My mother had immediately gone to the Red Cross office in the nearby city to learn how to send messages and packages. But why hadn't I ever answered any of the letters or even sent a note of thanks for the package she had mailed? I explained that I had sent both cards and letters home, but had never received mail from anyone, nor had any of the others in the room I lived in while there.

"Why not?"

"The Germans had more important things to do; they were trying to win a war."

"But they had to deliver the mail."

"They didn't have to do any of the usual or normal things, Mother. During a war, people do or don't do whatever helps them win."

She said she would try to understand that, but only because I said it was true — and I knew she would have trouble comprehending, and I knew I would have trouble communicating.

My fears were confirmed when I arrived at the village hall for the annual "family gathering," which had been scheduled for the following evening. A cousin excitedly explained he was canceling the few home-talent musical duets and solos that normally entertained the group because he knew everyone would rather hear about my experiences. He then asked the hundred relatives to take seats, repeated loudly what he had just said, and nodded toward me.

I knew I couldn't use any "bad words" to describe residual ill feelings about captors and incarceration without jeopardizing my membership in one of the four churches that served the village's eight hundred people. I also knew there wasn't time to edit thoughts about feelings and attitudes, so I merely briefly outlined the chronology of events since my leave the previous autumn.

When twenty minutes had elapsed with the story only half told, I further condensed the sequence to conclude within thirty minutes; it was like reading two or three sentences from every tenth page of this story. But when I finished everyone remained seated and snapped questions until I urged we conclude for the evening an hour later.

Because I was among the first to return from a war zone, there had been little chance for civilians to discuss these points with servicemen. Interests varied from curiosity about feelings and attitudes to issues of morality. One asked if had been fair of us to bomb the civilians in all of those cities.

I didn't blame anyone for asking any of the questions, but I felt my answers were always too brief and too undeveloped because others waited with different questions. After the morality concerns raised in the discussion that night, I slept as restlessly on a comfortable mattress as I had on boards while cold and hungry through nights when I thought my life was in danger in Germany.

Some of the questions were as innocent as mine had been when I wondered if men selected fields to do bloody things to each other while I was seven years old. I hadn't told them about the little pimp in Naples who had triggered that memory of those childhood thoughts. I hadn't told them that a leaping and flailing maniac in Vienna had called us "goddam pig-dog American terror fliers" while apparently feeling all of our bombings were very unfair.

I recalled again, as I had after gunnery training in Arizona, that the speaker hadn't talked about the war at our high school graduation just before the boys were inducted; he had selected a much easier subject from Joshua 1:8:

> . . . For then thou shalt make thy way prosperous, and then thou shalt have good success.

Later, as I looked for answers to some of the questions that had been raised about morality, I scanned further, and in Joshua 6:21, I found:

And they utterly destroyed all that was in the city, both man and woman, young and old, and ox, and sheep, and ass, with the edge of the sword.

In 8:25-26, I found:

. . . All that fell that day, both men and women, were twelve thousand. . . . For Joshua drew not his hand back, wherewith he stretched out the spear; until he had utterly destroyed all the inhabitants. . . .

Between those lines, I read that Joshua had had what seemed to be God's blessings or directions for his actions; all I had were my government's orders.

These verses had been around, however, for many hundreds of years through countless subsequent wars. Why did they now expect me to answer those difficult questions?

Furlough papers that had been hurriedly issued at Ft. Sheridan granted sixty days of complete freedom from military concerns. Service leaves of over a week or two had seldom been heard of before, but the medic there had explained that the extended period should allow a rehabilitation process to begin.

His concept of rehabilitation was interestingly different from what we had anticipated. I realized after the village hall gathering that I initially needed a temporary relief from the sordid thoughts about war. Former kriegies had found such relief in France, but it would be impossible here amid concerns about morality.

Use of a car and more cash than I had available would have allowed trips to entertainment in the city, but that seemed an artificial escape. Fortunately, a bumper crop of peas was being harvested from fields surrounding the village, and the local cannery needed all the seasonal helpers available; some employees worked more than twelve hours per day. The employment clerk said I could work as many hours as I wished, and I became preoccupied with canning processes from my first week at home until time to return to a military assignment. I needed to save earnings toward urgently needed additional education: I understood so few of the things I had seen.

An incident disturbed me on one of the first mornings while we waited for the cannery's starting whistle. A coworker pointed to six men on the next street corner and explained that they were German prisoners of war who had been brought from the internment center near the neighboring city; here, they were waiting for a truck to take them to harvesting jobs on local farms.

The coworker suggested I talk to them because both they and I would enjoy swapping stories. My supervisor agreed. I knew I wouldn't enjoy it, but I felt I shouldn't decline.

Curious looks on the Germans' faces as I approached turned to shocked stares when I announced, "Ich vas ine kriegsgefangenen in Doitchlant." After noticing my forced smile, they rattled more questions in German than I could understand. They switched to usable English when I explained that my capabilities with their language were limited. Initial interests concerned conditions of their hometowns: they didn't like my confirmations that the larger cities were mostly in ruins.

They were learning proper English usage because they enjoyed being here. They were treated well and had been warm and comfortable, healthy, well fed, and paid for their work. They all hoped to return to the States after being sent back to Germany; two of them said they were already saving their earnings for that purpose.

As I walked back to start my work day, I reasoned that each of them had seemed like a decent person, but my lingering resentments asked where the dogs were that should have been snarling at them, or the guards that should have been pointing guns at them and snickering about their predicament.

With my last week of work at the cannery approaching, I wondered if I would be retrained to fly in the Pacific war against the Japanese. A new and improved bomber, the B-29, with many advanced capabilities and a far greater flying range, had been developed and was being used in that area.

It had been over three and one-half years since America had said, "We'll beat 'em before breakfast," but no one expected an easy end there now. News analysts who had keenly honed their skills to ferret out the more reliable opinions wrote that losses from the massive D-day invasion might seem small when compared to estimated needs to invade Japan. Whispered guesses said a million Allied casualties might result, because the "hara-kiri behavior" would inspire Japanese military to give ten million lives to defend "the religious aspects of Japanese soil."

Radio announcements as confusing as those from the Pearl Harbor era almost four years earlier suddenly bewildered American listeners: we had dropped a bomb on Hiroshima.

"One bomb? Why not hundreds or thousands?"

"This was different. This was a new invention; a very powerful, new type of bomb, an 'atomic bomb.' "

"This was like many planes loaded full of bombs all put together into one gigantic bomb."

The United States warned Japan that a similar bomb would drop if she didn't surrender, and the second one dropped on Nagaski three days after the first. Japan then offered to discuss surrender terms, with the condition that she could retain her emperor.

Complying with previous military orders, I reported to Miami Beach, Florida, for "continued rehabilitation." There, in a hotel room on Collins Avenue, I listened to a radio announcer's play-by-play description of proceedings on the deck of the battleship *Missouri*, anchored in Tokyo Bay, of what some would call "the somewhat conditioned unconditional surrender."

After medical examinations, an updating of personal military records, and a violent September hurricane during the four weeks of recreation, I left for my next assignment as a squadron headquarters clerk at Truax Field near Madison, Wisconsin.

There was a favorable aspect of being back among servicemen: the communication barrier that many had experienced with hometown civilians had been left "back home." A need to apologetically explain reasons for ill feelings no longer existed; when European veterans met returnees from the Pacific Theater, we could tell them how the "damn Nazis" had treated us, and they could tell us what the "yellow bastards" had done to them.

After a few weeks, newscasters circulated exciting and plausible opinions that the nation would demobilize rapidly to save unnecessary military costs. There were rumors that Congress would support legislation for financial assistance toward continuing education, vocational training, and similar endeavors, to help reassimilation of thousands of veterans into the society from which they had been drawn. I wondered if I would be a normal civilian. I felt that additional schooling might best enhance my ability to fit into what, as predicted by many, would be "a different world."

Not yet aware that I would essentially remember everything from the war experience throughout all of my life, I was glad my mother had accumulated the huge box of clippings, so that I, much later, could analyze reasons for the thoughts that I then just wanted to put out of mind.

A plan soon developed that would facilitate an orderly discharge of servicemen based on points for seniority, flights, battles, and other factors credited to the individual's service record. Former prisoners of war, however, had neither advanced in rank nor accrued significant points during incarceration. A special system was therefore being considered for them based on POW records.

Two days after hearing about that consideration, I showed my discharge papers at the field exit gate and hitchhiked to my hometown, while suppressing the wildly exciting anticipation of a new era of freedom and choice.

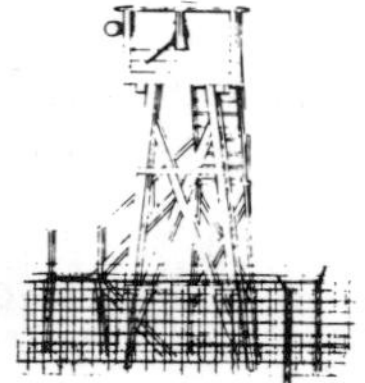

Epilogue

For the reader, that is the end of this story of just another war, as remembered by one of the many millions of people involved in it around the world.

For the writer, the story didn't end there; most of its facets remained near the surface of a random-access memory for the half-century that has since elapsed.

During the first months, while the veterans were trying to become useful civilians, we were told we had won the war, now we must win the peace. I added to the congestion in lecture halls and laboratories, like many thousands of other former-soldier-students. We read newspaper reports later that our professors enjoyed our determination to acquire and apply knowledge.

I went to Oregon during one summer for a first meeting with the uncle who had fought in the trenches of France three decades earlier and had written the profoundly insightful letter to me during my gunnery school training. We compared differences between our wars with just a few words, and we understood similarities without discussion.

We agreed that some of the people we had returned to wondered if we had been adequately gentle to those we had been ordered to kill. I mused that the bayonets of those who wondered would not have gone through a bag of sticks; how could they injure the feelings of those who had tried to help win the peace?

America was retooling to convert a wartime economy to peacetime efforts and to replenish goods and gadgets for anxious consumers. As I searched for work, a new war for our country was starting in Korea, but our people couldn't agree on whether it should be called a war or a conflict, and its economic impact wasn't large enough to redirect domestic efforts. Our country became involved in still another war effort within the second decade after my war. This time I was an uncle with a nephew in Vietnam, and some of our people couldn't agree that we should all support that effort.

Business had been excellent, and the company I worked for built a new headquarters complex with a flagpole at each side of the main entrance. The American flag was displayed on one and our State flag on the other; on days when foreign customers visited, the flag of their country replaced that of our State.

After several weeks in our new building, a man I knew from the maintenance department walked into my office looking ill or frightened before the work day started. "I'll be fine," he assured, "I just had a weird experience and wanted to talk to somebody who'd understand.

"I feel like a traitor," he explained. "It was my job a few minutes ago to pull that damn Rising Sun up, right along beside Ol' Glory. You know, only a few years back, it was my patriotic duty to tear their damn rags down. Don't tell anybody I said so, but it's an odd feeling. Do you understand?"

I assured him sincerely that I understood — and I never told anyone he had said those things.

A few years later, I was stopped in an aisle to settle a disagreement between two bright young coworkers. One said, "This has nothing to do with work; we just got onto another subject for a minute. Did Hitler croak before the bomb dropped or after?" Hoping to encourage further thought, I quipped, "Which bomb? There were millions, you know."

He grinned wryly and said, "Look, we don't have time for that; everybody knows only one bomb made any real difference in that war." I didn't have time either, and I realized as I walked down the aisle that, being over fifteen years younger than I, they had been preschool toddlers when my war ended.

Before forty years had elapsed after that war, a man in his forties emphasized a point in a speech with, "It's only a few decades ago that Winston Churchill said, 'The only thing we have to fear is fear itself.' " Many in the audience were embarrassed, because most of us in our fifties remembered that President Roosevelt had said that, and for a very different reason than that cited. I wondered whether the important things we thought we had learned in the World War II era had now been forgotten.

In a discussion group that coincidentally met on an anniversary of the bombing of Hiroshima some thirty years after World War II had ended, a man suggested we close our meeting with one-line prayers from anyone wishing to participate. He then offered: "Forgive us, Lord, for being the country that dropped the bomb that killed eighty thousand people."

As I pondered his prayer later, I remembered reports that President Truman had agonized over the final decision of whether or not to use the atomic bomb. Previous estimates had predicted that ten million Japanese would die if we had alternatively invaded their country to end the war with conventional means. Odds favored the bomb by over ninety-five percent.

I wondered if we would have needed ten times as much forgiveness if we had killed the additional 9.9 million instead.

Despite questions that persisted and concerns that developed after 1945, there was widespread acceptance of our government's policies and of the decisions and actions of our military forces. One of our soldiers came home, became the country's President, and later advocated that, in our pledge of allegiance to the nation, we add the words "under God."

Index

Compiled by Ginger Weir